C-4597　　CAREER EXAMINATION SERIES

This is your
PASSBOOK for...

Firefighter Entry Aptitude Test (FEAT)

Test Preparation Study Guide
Questions & Answers

NATIONAL LEARNING CORPORATION®

COPYRIGHT NOTICE

This book is SOLELY intended for, is sold ONLY to, and its use is RESTRICTED to individual, bona fide applicants or candidates who qualify by virtue of having seriously filed applications for appropriate license, certificate, professional and/or promotional advancement, higher school matriculation, scholarship, or other legitimate requirements of education and/or governmental authorities.

This book is NOT intended for use, class instruction, tutoring, training, duplication, copying, reprinting, excerption, or adaptation, etc., by:

1) Other publishers
2) Proprietors and/or Instructors of "Coaching" and/or Preparatory Courses
3) Personnel and/or Training Divisions of commercial, industrial, and governmental organizations
4) Schools, colleges, or universities and/or their departments and staffs, including teachers and other personnel
5) Testing Agencies or Bureaus
6) Study groups which seek by the purchase of a single volume to copy and/or duplicate and/or adapt this material for use by the group as a whole without having purchased individual volumes for each of the members of the group
7) Et al.

Such persons would be in violation of appropriate Federal and State statutes.

PROVISION OF LICENSING AGREEMENTS – Recognized educational, commercial, industrial, and governmental institutions and organizations, and others legitimately engaged in educational pursuits, including training, testing, and measurement activities, may address request for a licensing agreement to the copyright owners, who will determine whether, and under what conditions, including fees and charges, the materials in this book may be used them. In other words, a licensing facility exists for the legitimate use of the material in this book on other than an individual basis. However, it is asseverated and affirmed here that the material in this book CANNOT be used without the receipt of the express permission of such a licensing agreement from the Publishers. Inquiries re licensing should be addressed to the company, attention rights and permissions department.

All rights reserved, including the right of reproduction in whole or in part, in any form or by any means, electronic or mechanical, including photocopying, recording, or by any information storage and retrieval system, without permission in writing from the Publisher.

Copyright © 2024 by
National Learning Corporation

212 Michael Drive, Syosset, NY 11791
(516) 921-8888 • www.passbooks.com
E-mail: info@passbooks.com

PUBLISHED IN THE UNITED STATES OF AMERICA

PASSBOOK® SERIES

THE *PASSBOOK® SERIES* has been created to prepare applicants and candidates for the ultimate academic battlefield – the examination room.

At some time in our lives, each and every one of us may be required to take an examination – for validation, matriculation, admission, qualification, registration, certification, or licensure.

Based on the assumption that every applicant or candidate has met the basic formal educational standards, has taken the required number of courses, and read the necessary texts, the *PASSBOOK® SERIES* furnishes the one special preparation which may assure passing with confidence, instead of failing with insecurity. Examination questions – together with answers – are furnished as the basic vehicle for study so that the mysteries of the examination and its compounding difficulties may be eliminated or diminished by a sure method.

This book is meant to help you pass your examination provided that you qualify and are serious in your objective.

The entire field is reviewed through the huge store of content information which is succinctly presented through a provocative and challenging approach – the question-and-answer method.

A climate of success is established by furnishing the correct answers at the end of each test.

You soon learn to recognize types of questions, forms of questions, and patterns of questioning. You may even begin to anticipate expected outcomes.

You perceive that many questions are repeated or adapted so that you can gain acute insights, which may enable you to score many sure points.

You learn how to confront new questions, or types of questions, and to attack them confidently and work out the correct answers.

You note objectives and emphases, and recognize pitfalls and dangers, so that you may make positive educational adjustments.

Moreover, you are kept fully informed in relation to new concepts, methods, practices, and directions in the field.

You discover that you are actually taking the examination all the time: you are preparing for the examination by "taking" an examination, not by reading extraneous and/or supererogatory textbooks.

In short, this PASSBOOK®, used directedly, should be an important factor in helping you to pass your test.

FIREFIGHTER ENTRY APTITUDE TEST

ABOUT THE EXAM

The Firefighter Entry Aptitude Test is a cognitive test of selected knowledge, skills and aptitudes necessary to succeed as a Firefighter in today's environment. It consists of approximately 100 questions, divided into sections to gauge the candidate's understanding of written and oral information, arithmetical reasoning, maps, diagrams and mechanical drawings. It must be compelted within a set time limit. Applicants must obtain a score established by the city to pass the test to be eligible to proceed to the next step in the recruitment process.

HOW TO TAKE A TEST

I. YOU MUST PASS AN EXAMINATION

A. *WHAT EVERY CANDIDATE SHOULD KNOW*

Examination applicants often ask us for help in preparing for the written test. What can I study in advance? What kinds of questions will be asked? How will the test be given? How will the papers be graded?

As an applicant for a civil service examination, you may be wondering about some of these things. Our purpose here is to suggest effective methods of advance study and to describe civil service examinations.

Your chances for success on this examination can be increased if you know how to prepare. Those "pre-examination jitters" can be reduced if you know what to expect. You can even experience an adventure in good citizenship if you know why civil service exams are given.

B. *WHY ARE CIVIL SERVICE EXAMINATIONS GIVEN?*

Civil service examinations are important to you in two ways. As a citizen, you want public jobs filled by employees who know how to do their work. As a job seeker, you want a fair chance to compete for that job on an equal footing with other candidates. The best-known means of accomplishing this two-fold goal is the competitive examination.

Exams are widely publicized throughout the nation. They may be administered for jobs in federal, state, city, municipal, town or village governments or agencies.

Any citizen may apply, with some limitations, such as the age or residence of applicants. Your experience and education may be reviewed to see whether you meet the requirements for the particular examination. When these requirements exist, they are reasonable and applied consistently to all applicants. Thus, a competitive examination may cause you some uneasiness now, but it is your privilege and safeguard.

C. *HOW ARE CIVIL SERVICE EXAMS DEVELOPED?*

Examinations are carefully written by trained technicians who are specialists in the field known as "psychological measurement," in consultation with recognized authorities in the field of work that the test will cover. These experts recommend the subject matter areas or skills to be tested; only those knowledges or skills important to your success on the job are included. The most reliable books and source materials available are used as references. Together, the experts and technicians judge the difficulty level of the questions.

Test technicians know how to phrase questions so that the problem is clearly stated. Their ethics do not permit "trick" or "catch" questions. Questions may have been tried out on sample groups, or subjected to statistical analysis, to determine their usefulness.

Written tests are often used in combination with performance tests, ratings of training and experience, and oral interviews. All of these measures combine to form the best-known means of finding the right person for the right job.

II. HOW TO PASS THE WRITTEN TEST

A. NATURE OF THE EXAMINATION

To prepare intelligently for civil service examinations, you should know how they differ from school examinations you have taken. In school you were assigned certain definite pages to read or subjects to cover. The examination questions were quite detailed and usually emphasized memory. Civil service exams, on the other hand, try to discover your present ability to perform the duties of a position, plus your potentiality to learn these duties. In other words, a civil service exam attempts to predict how successful you will be. Questions cover such a broad area that they cannot be as minute and detailed as school exam questions.

In the public service similar kinds of work, or positions, are grouped together in one "class." This process is known as *position-classification*. All the positions in a class are paid according to the salary range for that class. One class title covers all of these positions, and they are all tested by the same examination.

B. FOUR BASIC STEPS

1) Study the announcement

How, then, can you know what subjects to study? Our best answer is: "Learn as much as possible about the class of positions for which you've applied." The exam will test the knowledge, skills and abilities needed to do the work.

Your most valuable source of information about the position you want is the official exam announcement. This announcement lists the training and experience qualifications. Check these standards and apply only if you come reasonably close to meeting them.

The brief description of the position in the examination announcement offers some clues to the subjects which will be tested. Think about the job itself. Review the duties in your mind. Can you perform them, or are there some in which you are rusty? Fill in the blank spots in your preparation.

Many jurisdictions preview the written test in the exam announcement by including a section called "Knowledge and Abilities Required," "Scope of the Examination," or some similar heading. Here you will find out specifically what fields will be tested.

2) Review your own background

Once you learn in general what the position is all about, and what you need to know to do the work, ask yourself which subjects you already know fairly well and which need improvement. You may wonder whether to concentrate on improving your strong areas or on building some background in your fields of weakness. When the announcement has specified "some knowledge" or "considerable knowledge," or has used adjectives like "beginning principles of..." or "advanced ... methods," you can get a clue as to the number and difficulty of questions to be asked in any given field. More questions, and hence broader coverage, would be included for those subjects which are more important in the work. Now weigh your strengths and weaknesses against the job requirements and prepare accordingly.

3) Determine the level of the position

Another way to tell how intensively you should prepare is to understand the level of the job for which you are applying. Is it the entering level? In other words, is this the position in which beginners in a field of work are hired? Or is it an intermediate or advanced level? Sometimes this is indicated by such words as "Junior" or "Senior" in the class title. Other jurisdictions use Roman numerals to designate the level – Clerk I, Clerk II, for example. The word "Supervisor" sometimes appears in the title. If the level is not indicated by the title, check the description of duties. Will you be working under very close supervision, or will you have responsibility for independent decisions in this work?

4) Choose appropriate study materials

Now that you know the subjects to be examined and the relative amount of each subject to be covered, you can choose suitable study materials. For beginning level jobs, or even advanced ones, if you have a pronounced weakness in some aspect of your training, read a modern, standard textbook in that field. Be sure it is up to date and has general coverage. Such books are normally available at your library, and the librarian will be glad to help you locate one. For entry-level positions, questions of appropriate difficulty are chosen — neither highly advanced questions, nor those too simple. Such questions require careful thought but not advanced training.

If the position for which you are applying is technical or advanced, you will read more advanced, specialized material. If you are already familiar with the basic principles of your field, elementary textbooks would waste your time. Concentrate on advanced textbooks and technical periodicals. Think through the concepts and review difficult problems in your field.

These are all general sources. You can get more ideas on your own initiative, following these leads. For example, training manuals and publications of the government agency which employs workers in your field can be useful, particularly for technical and professional positions. A letter or visit to the government department involved may result in more specific study suggestions, and certainly will provide you with a more definite idea of the exact nature of the position you are seeking.

III. KINDS OF TESTS

Tests are used for purposes other than measuring knowledge and ability to perform specified duties. For some positions, it is equally important to test ability to make adjustments to new situations or to profit from training. In others, basic mental abilities not dependent on information are essential. Questions which test these things may not appear as pertinent to the duties of the position as those which test for knowledge and information. Yet they are often highly important parts of a fair examination. For very general questions, it is almost impossible to help you direct your study efforts. What we can do is to point out some of the more common of these general abilities needed in public service positions and describe some typical questions.

1) General information

Broad, general information has been found useful for predicting job success in some kinds of work. This is tested in a variety of ways, from vocabulary lists to questions about current events. Basic background in some field of work, such as sociology or economics, may be sampled in a group of questions. Often these are principles which have become familiar to most persons through exposure rather than through formal training. It is difficult to advise you how to study for these questions; being alert to the world around you is our best suggestion.

2) Verbal ability

An example of an ability needed in many positions is verbal or language ability. Verbal ability is, in brief, the ability to use and understand words. Vocabulary and grammar tests are typical measures of this ability. Reading comprehension or paragraph interpretation questions are common in many kinds of civil service tests. You are given a paragraph of written material and asked to find its central meaning.

3) Numerical ability

Number skills can be tested by the familiar arithmetic problem, by checking paired lists of numbers to see which are alike and which are different, or by interpreting charts and graphs. In the latter test, a graph may be printed in the test booklet which you are asked to use as the basis for answering questions.

4) Observation

A popular test for law-enforcement positions is the observation test. A picture is shown to you for several minutes, then taken away. Questions about the picture test your ability to observe both details and larger elements.

5) Following directions

In many positions in the public service, the employee must be able to carry out written instructions dependably and accurately. You may be given a chart with several columns, each column listing a variety of information. The questions require you to carry out directions involving the information given in the chart.

6) Skills and aptitudes

Performance tests effectively measure some manual skills and aptitudes. When the skill is one in which you are trained, such as typing or shorthand, you can practice. These tests are often very much like those given in business school or high school courses. For many of the other skills and aptitudes, however, no short-time preparation can be made. Skills and abilities natural to you or that you have developed throughout your lifetime are being tested.

Many of the general questions just described provide all the data needed to answer the questions and ask you to use your reasoning ability to find the answers. Your best preparation for these tests, as well as for tests of facts and ideas, is to be at your physical and mental best. You, no doubt, have your own methods of getting into an exam-taking mood and keeping "in shape." The next section lists some ideas on this subject.

IV. KINDS OF QUESTIONS

Only rarely is the "essay" question, which you answer in narrative form, used in civil service tests. Civil service tests are usually of the short-answer type. Full instructions for answering these questions will be given to you at the examination. But in case this is your first experience with short-answer questions and separate answer sheets, here is what you need to know:

1) Multiple-choice Questions

Most popular of the short-answer questions is the "multiple choice" or "best answer" question. It can be used, for example, to test for factual knowledge, ability to solve problems or judgment in meeting situations found at work.

A multiple-choice question is normally one of three types—
- It can begin with an incomplete statement followed by several possible endings. You are to find the one ending which *best* completes the statement, although some of the others may not be entirely wrong.
- It can also be a complete statement in the form of a question which is answered by choosing one of the statements listed.

- It can be in the form of a problem – again you select the best answer.

Here is an example of a multiple-choice question with a discussion which should give you some clues as to the method for choosing the right answer:

When an employee has a complaint about his assignment, the action which will *best* help him overcome his difficulty is to
- A. discuss his difficulty with his coworkers
- B. take the problem to the head of the organization
- C. take the problem to the person who gave him the assignment
- D. say nothing to anyone about his complaint

In answering this question, you should study each of the choices to find which is best. Consider choice "A" – Certainly an employee may discuss his complaint with fellow employees, but no change or improvement can result, and the complaint remains unresolved. Choice "B" is a poor choice since the head of the organization probably does not know what assignment you have been given, and taking your problem to him is known as "going over the head" of the supervisor. The supervisor, or person who made the assignment, is the person who can clarify it or correct any injustice. Choice "C" is, therefore, correct. To say nothing, as in choice "D," is unwise. Supervisors have and interest in knowing the problems employees are facing, and the employee is seeking a solution to his problem.

2) True/False Questions

The "true/false" or "right/wrong" form of question is sometimes used. Here a complete statement is given. Your job is to decide whether the statement is right or wrong.

SAMPLE: A roaming cell-phone call to a nearby city costs less than a non-roaming call to a distant city.

This statement is wrong, or false, since roaming calls are more expensive.

This is not a complete list of all possible question forms, although most of the others are variations of these common types. You will always get complete directions for answering questions. Be sure you understand *how* to mark your answers – ask questions until you do.

V. RECORDING YOUR ANSWERS

Computer terminals are used more and more today for many different kinds of exams.
For an examination with very few applicants, you may be told to record your answers in the test booklet itself. Separate answer sheets are much more common. If this separate answer sheet is to be scored by machine – and this is often the case – it is highly important that you mark your answers correctly in order to get credit.

An electronic scoring machine is often used in civil service offices because of the speed with which papers can be scored. Machine-scored answer sheets must be marked with a pencil, which will be given to you. This pencil has a high graphite content which responds to the electronic scoring machine. As a matter of fact, stray dots may register as answers, so do not let your pencil rest on the answer sheet while you are pondering the correct answer. Also, if your pencil lead breaks or is otherwise defective, ask for another.

Since the answer sheet will be dropped in a slot in the scoring machine, be careful not to bend the corners or get the paper crumpled.

The answer sheet normally has five vertical columns of numbers, with 30 numbers to a column. These numbers correspond to the question numbers in your test booklet. After each number, going across the page are four or five pairs of dotted lines. These short dotted lines have small letters or numbers above them. The first two pairs may also have a "T" or "F" above the letters. This indicates that the first two pairs only are to be used if the questions are of the true-false type. If the questions are multiple choice, disregard the "T" and "F" and pay attention only to the small letters or numbers.

Answer your questions in the manner of the sample that follows:

32. The largest city in the United States is
    A. Washington, D.C.
    B. New York City
    C. Chicago
    D. Detroit
    E. San Francisco

1) Choose the answer you think is best. (New York City is the largest, so "B" is correct.)
2) Find the row of dotted lines numbered the same as the question you are answering. (Find row number 32)
3) Find the pair of dotted lines corresponding to the answer. (Find the pair of lines under the mark "B.")
4) Make a solid black mark between the dotted lines.

VI. BEFORE THE TEST

Common sense will help you find procedures to follow to get ready for an examination. Too many of us, however, overlook these sensible measures. Indeed, nervousness and fatigue have been found to be the most serious reasons why applicants fail to do their best on civil service tests. Here is a list of reminders:

- Begin your preparation early – Don't wait until the last minute to go scurrying around for books and materials or to find out what the position is all about.
- Prepare continuously – An hour a night for a week is better than an all-night cram session. This has been definitely established. What is more, a night a week for a month will return better dividends than crowding your study into a shorter period of time.
- Locate the place of the exam – You have been sent a notice telling you when and where to report for the examination. If the location is in a different town or otherwise unfamiliar to you, it would be well to inquire the best route and learn something about the building.
- Relax the night before the test – Allow your mind to rest. Do not study at all that night. Plan some mild recreation or diversion; then go to bed early and get a good night's sleep.
- Get up early enough to make a leisurely trip to the place for the test – This way unforeseen events, traffic snarls, unfamiliar buildings, etc. will not upset you.
- Dress comfortably – A written test is not a fashion show. You will be known by number and not by name, so wear something comfortable.

- Leave excess paraphernalia at home – Shopping bags and odd bundles will get in your way. You need bring only the items mentioned in the official notice you received; usually everything you need is provided. Do not bring reference books to the exam. They will only confuse those last minutes and be taken away from you when in the test room.
- Arrive somewhat ahead of time – If because of transportation schedules you must get there very early, bring a newspaper or magazine to take your mind off yourself while waiting.
- Locate the examination room – When you have found the proper room, you will be directed to the seat or part of the room where you will sit. Sometimes you are given a sheet of instructions to read while you are waiting. Do not fill out any forms until you are told to do so; just read them and be prepared.
- Relax and prepare to listen to the instructions
- If you have any physical problem that may keep you from doing your best, be sure to tell the test administrator. If you are sick or in poor health, you really cannot do your best on the exam. You can come back and take the test some other time.

VII. AT THE TEST

The day of the test is here and you have the test booklet in your hand. The temptation to get going is very strong. Caution! There is more to success than knowing the right answers. You must know how to identify your papers and understand variations in the type of short-answer question used in this particular examination. Follow these suggestions for maximum results from your efforts:

1) Cooperate with the monitor

The test administrator has a duty to create a situation in which you can be as much at ease as possible. He will give instructions, tell you when to begin, check to see that you are marking your answer sheet correctly, and so on. He is not there to guard you, although he will see that your competitors do not take unfair advantage. He wants to help you do your best.

2) Listen to all instructions

Don't jump the gun! Wait until you understand all directions. In most civil service tests you get more time than you need to answer the questions. So don't be in a hurry. Read each word of instructions until you clearly understand the meaning. Study the examples, listen to all announcements and follow directions. Ask questions if you do not understand what to do.

3) Identify your papers

Civil service exams are usually identified by number only. You will be assigned a number; you must not put your name on your test papers. Be sure to copy your number correctly. Since more than one exam may be given, copy your exact examination title.

4) Plan your time

Unless you are told that a test is a "speed" or "rate of work" test, speed itself is usually not important. Time enough to answer all the questions will be provided, but this does not mean that you have all day. An overall time limit has been set. Divide the total time (in minutes) by the number of questions to determine the approximate time you have for each question.

5) Do not linger over difficult questions

If you come across a difficult question, mark it with a paper clip (useful to have along) and come back to it when you have been through the booklet. One caution if you do this – be sure to skip a number on your answer sheet as well. Check often to be sure that you have not lost your place and that you are marking in the row numbered the same as the question you are answering.

6) Read the questions

Be sure you know what the question asks! Many capable people are unsuccessful because they failed to *read* the questions correctly.

7) Answer all questions

Unless you have been instructed that a penalty will be deducted for incorrect answers, it is better to guess than to omit a question.

8) Speed tests

It is often better NOT to guess on speed tests. It has been found that on timed tests people are tempted to spend the last few seconds before time is called in marking answers at random – without even reading them – in the hope of picking up a few extra points. To discourage this practice, the instructions may warn you that your score will be "corrected" for guessing. That is, a penalty will be applied. The incorrect answers will be deducted from the correct ones, or some other penalty formula will be used.

9) Review your answers

If you finish before time is called, go back to the questions you guessed or omitted to give them further thought. Review other answers if you have time.

10) Return your test materials

If you are ready to leave before others have finished or time is called, take ALL your materials to the monitor and leave quietly. Never take any test material with you. The monitor can discover whose papers are not complete, and taking a test booklet may be grounds for disqualification.

VIII. EXAMINATION TECHNIQUES

1) Read the general instructions carefully. These are usually printed on the first page of the exam booklet. As a rule, these instructions refer to the timing of the examination; the fact that you should not start work until the signal and must stop work at a signal, etc. If there are any *special* instructions, such as a choice of questions to be answered, make sure that you note this instruction carefully.

2) When you are ready to start work on the examination, that is as soon as the signal has been given, read the instructions to each question booklet, underline any key words or phrases, such as *least, best, outline, describe* and the like. In this way you will tend to answer as requested rather than discover on reviewing your paper that you *listed without describing*, that you selected the *worst* choice rather than the *best* choice, etc.

3) If the examination is of the objective or multiple-choice type – that is, each question will also give a series of possible answers: A, B, C or D, and you are called upon to select the best answer and write the letter next to that answer on your answer paper – it is advisable to start answering each question in turn. There may be anywhere from 50 to 100 such questions in the three or four hours allotted and you can see how much time would be taken if you read through all the questions before beginning to answer any. Furthermore, if you come across a question or group of questions which you know would be difficult to answer, it would undoubtedly affect your handling of all the other questions.

4) If the examination is of the essay type and contains but a few questions, it is a moot point as to whether you should read all the questions before starting to answer any one. Of course, if you are given a choice – say five out of seven and the like – then it is essential to read all the questions so you can eliminate the two that are most difficult. If, however, you are asked to answer all the questions, there may be danger in trying to answer the easiest one first because you may find that you will spend too much time on it. The best technique is to answer the first question, then proceed to the second, etc.

5) Time your answers. Before the exam begins, write down the time it started, then add the time allowed for the examination and write down the time it must be completed, then divide the time available somewhat as follows:
    - If 3-1/2 hours are allowed, that would be 210 minutes. If you have 80 objective-type questions, that would be an average of 2-1/2 minutes per question. Allow yourself no more than 2 minutes per question, or a total of 160 minutes, which will permit about 50 minutes to review.
    - If for the time allotment of 210 minutes there are 7 essay questions to answer, that would average about 30 minutes a question. Give yourself only 25 minutes per question so that you have about 35 minutes to review.

6) The most important instruction is to *read each question* and make sure you know what is wanted. The second most important instruction is to *time yourself properly* so that you answer every question. The third most important instruction is to *answer every question*. Guess if you have to but include something for each question. Remember that you will receive no credit for a blank and will probably receive some credit if you write something in answer to an essay question. If you guess a letter – say "B" for a multiple-choice question – you may have guessed right. If you leave a blank as an answer to a multiple-choice question, the examiners may respect your feelings but it will not add a point to your score. Some exams may penalize you for wrong answers, so in such cases *only*, you may not want to guess unless you have some basis for your answer.

7) Suggestions
    a. Objective-type questions
        1. Examine the question booklet for proper sequence of pages and questions
        2. Read all instructions carefully
        3. Skip any question which seems too difficult; return to it after all other questions have been answered
        4. Apportion your time properly; do not spend too much time on any single question or group of questions

5. Note and underline key words – *all, most, fewest, least, best, worst, same, opposite*, etc.
6. Pay particular attention to negatives
7. Note unusual option, e.g., unduly long, short, complex, different or similar in content to the body of the question
8. Observe the use of "hedging" words – *probably, may, most likely*, etc.
9. Make sure that your answer is put next to the same number as the question
10. Do not second-guess unless you have good reason to believe the second answer is definitely more correct
11. Cross out original answer if you decide another answer is more accurate; do not erase until you are ready to hand your paper in
12. Answer all questions; guess unless instructed otherwise
13. Leave time for review

   b. Essay questions
   1. Read each question carefully
   2. Determine exactly what is wanted. Underline key words or phrases.
   3. Decide on outline or paragraph answer
   4. Include many different points and elements unless asked to develop any one or two points or elements
   5. Show impartiality by giving pros and cons unless directed to select one side only
   6. Make and write down any assumptions you find necessary to answer the questions
   7. Watch your English, grammar, punctuation and choice of words
   8. Time your answers; don't crowd material

8) Answering the essay question

Most essay questions can be answered by framing the specific response around several key words or ideas. Here are a few such key words or ideas:

M's: manpower, materials, methods, money, management
P's: purpose, program, policy, plan, procedure, practice, problems, pitfalls, personnel, public relations
   a. Six basic steps in handling problems:
   1. Preliminary plan and background development
   2. Collect information, data and facts
   3. Analyze and interpret information, data and facts
   4. Analyze and develop solutions as well as make recommendations
   5. Prepare report and sell recommendations
   6. Install recommendations and follow up effectiveness

   b. Pitfalls to avoid
   1. *Taking things for granted* – A statement of the situation does not necessarily imply that each of the elements is necessarily true; for example, a complaint may be invalid and biased so that all that can be taken for granted is that a complaint has been registered

2. *Considering only one side of a situation* – Wherever possible, indicate several alternatives and then point out the reasons you selected the best one
3. *Failing to indicate follow up* – Whenever your answer indicates action on your part, make certain that you will take proper follow-up action to see how successful your recommendations, procedures or actions turn out to be
4. *Taking too long in answering any single question* – Remember to time your answers properly

IX. AFTER THE TEST

Scoring procedures differ in detail among civil service jurisdictions although the general principles are the same. Whether the papers are hand-scored or graded by machine we have described, they are nearly always graded by number. That is, the person who marks the paper knows only the number – never the name – of the applicant. Not until all the papers have been graded will they be matched with names. If other tests, such as training and experience or oral interview ratings have been given, scores will be combined. Different parts of the examination usually have different weights. For example, the written test might count 60 percent of the final grade, and a rating of training and experience 40 percent. In many jurisdictions, veterans will have a certain number of points added to their grades.

After the final grade has been determined, the names are placed in grade order and an eligible list is established. There are various methods for resolving ties between those who get the same final grade – probably the most common is to place first the name of the person whose application was received first. Job offers are made from the eligible list in the order the names appear on it. You will be notified of your grade and your rank as soon as all these computations have been made. This will be done as rapidly as possible.

People who are found to meet the requirements in the announcement are called "eligibles." Their names are put on a list of eligible candidates. An eligible's chances of getting a job depend on how high he stands on this list and how fast agencies are filling jobs from the list.

When a job is to be filled from a list of eligibles, the agency asks for the names of people on the list of eligibles for that job. When the civil service commission receives this request, it sends to the agency the names of the three people highest on this list. Or, if the job to be filled has specialized requirements, the office sends the agency the names of the top three persons who meet these requirements from the general list.

The appointing officer makes a choice from among the three people whose names were sent to him. If the selected person accepts the appointment, the names of the others are put back on the list to be considered for future openings.

That is the rule in hiring from all kinds of eligible lists, whether they are for typist, carpenter, chemist, or something else. For every vacancy, the appointing officer has his choice of any one of the top three eligibles on the list. This explains why the person whose name is on top of the list sometimes does not get an appointment when some of the persons lower on the list do. If the appointing officer chooses the second or third eligible, the No. 1 eligible does not get a job at once, but stays on the list until he is appointed or the list is terminated.

X. HOW TO PASS THE INTERVIEW TEST

The examination for which you applied requires an oral interview test. You have already taken the written test and you are now being called for the interview test – the final part of the formal examination.

You may think that it is not possible to prepare for an interview test and that there are no procedures to follow during an interview. Our purpose is to point out some things you can do in advance that will help you and some good rules to follow and pitfalls to avoid while you are being interviewed.

What is an interview supposed to test?

The written examination is designed to test the technical knowledge and competence of the candidate; the oral is designed to evaluate intangible qualities, not readily measured otherwise, and to establish a list showing the relative fitness of each candidate – as measured against his competitors – for the position sought. Scoring is not on the basis of "right" and "wrong," but on a sliding scale of values ranging from "not passable" to "outstanding." As a matter of fact, it is possible to achieve a relatively low score without a single "incorrect" answer because of evident weakness in the qualities being measured.

Occasionally, an examination may consist entirely of an oral test – either an individual or a group oral. In such cases, information is sought concerning the technical knowledges and abilities of the candidate, since there has been no written examination for this purpose. More commonly, however, an oral test is used to supplement a written examination.

Who conducts interviews?

The composition of oral boards varies among different jurisdictions. In nearly all, a representative of the personnel department serves as chairman. One of the members of the board may be a representative of the department in which the candidate would work. In some cases, "outside experts" are used, and, frequently, a businessman or some other representative of the general public is asked to serve. Labor and management or other special groups may be represented. The aim is to secure the services of experts in the appropriate field.

However the board is composed, it is a good idea (and not at all improper or unethical) to ascertain in advance of the interview who the members are and what groups they represent. When you are introduced to them, you will have some idea of their backgrounds and interests, and at least you will not stutter and stammer over their names.

What should be done before the interview?

While knowledge about the board members is useful and takes some of the surprise element out of the interview, there is other preparation which is more substantive. It *is* possible to prepare for an oral interview – in several ways:

1) Keep a copy of your application and review it carefully before the interview

This may be the only document before the oral board, and the starting point of the interview. Know what education and experience you have listed there, and the sequence and dates of all of it. Sometimes the board will ask you to review the highlights of your experience for them; you should not have to hem and haw doing it.

2) Study the class specification and the examination announcement

Usually, the oral board has one or both of these to guide them. The qualities, characteristics or knowledges required by the position sought are stated in these documents. They offer valuable clues as to the nature of the oral interview. For example, if the job involves supervisory responsibilities, the announcement will usually indicate that knowledge of modern supervisory methods and the qualifications of the candidate as a supervisor will be tested. If so, you can expect such questions, frequently in the form of a hypothetical situation which you are expected to solve. NEVER go into an oral without knowledge of the duties and responsibilities of the job you seek.

3) Think through each qualification required

Try to visualize the kind of questions you would ask if you were a board member. How well could you answer them? Try especially to appraise your own knowledge and background in each area, *measured against the job sought*, and identify any areas in which you are weak. Be critical and realistic – do not flatter yourself.

4) Do some general reading in areas in which you feel you may be weak

For example, if the job involves supervision and your past experience has NOT, some general reading in supervisory methods and practices, particularly in the field of human relations, might be useful. Do NOT study agency procedures or detailed manuals. The oral board will be testing your understanding and capacity, not your memory.

5) Get a good night's sleep and watch your general health and mental attitude

You will want a clear head at the interview. Take care of a cold or any other minor ailment, and of course, no hangovers.

What should be done on the day of the interview?

Now comes the day of the interview itself. Give yourself plenty of time to get there. Plan to arrive somewhat ahead of the scheduled time, particularly if your appointment is in the fore part of the day. If a previous candidate fails to appear, the board might be ready for you a bit early. By early afternoon an oral board is almost invariably behind schedule if there are many candidates, and you may have to wait. Take along a book or magazine to read, or your application to review, but leave any extraneous material in the waiting room when you go in for your interview. In any event, relax and compose yourself.

The matter of dress is important. The board is forming impressions about you – from your experience, your manners, your attitude, and your appearance. Give your personal appearance careful attention. Dress your best, but not your flashiest. Choose conservative, appropriate clothing, and be sure it is immaculate. This is a business interview, and your appearance should indicate that you regard it as such. Besides, being well groomed and properly dressed will help boost your confidence.

Sooner or later, someone will call your name and escort you into the interview room. *This is it.* From here on you are on your own. It is too late for any more preparation. But remember, you asked for this opportunity to prove your fitness, and you are here because your request was granted.

What happens when you go in?

The usual sequence of events will be as follows: The clerk (who is often the board stenographer) will introduce you to the chairman of the oral board, who will introduce you to the other members of the board. Acknowledge the introductions before you sit down. Do not be surprised if you find a microphone facing you or a stenotypist sitting by. Oral interviews are usually recorded in the event of an appeal or other review.

Usually the chairman of the board will open the interview by reviewing the highlights of your education and work experience from your application – primarily for the benefit of the other members of the board, as well as to get the material into the record. Do not interrupt or comment unless there is an error or significant misinterpretation; if that is the case, do not hesitate. But do not quibble about insignificant matters. Also, he will usually ask you some question about your education, experience or your present job – partly to get you to start talking and to establish the interviewing "rapport." He may start the actual questioning, or turn it over to one of the other members. Frequently, each member undertakes the questioning on a particular area, one in which he is perhaps most competent, so you can expect each member to participate in the examination. Because time is limited, you may also expect some rather abrupt switches in the direction the questioning takes, so do not be upset by it. Normally, a board member will not pursue a single line of questioning unless he discovers a particular strength or weakness.

After each member has participated, the chairman will usually ask whether any member has any further questions, then will ask you if you have anything you wish to add. Unless you are expecting this question, it may floor you. Worse, it may start you off on an extended, extemporaneous speech. The board is not usually seeking more information. The question is principally to offer you a last opportunity to present further qualifications or to indicate that you have nothing to add. So, if you feel that a significant qualification or characteristic has been overlooked, it is proper to point it out in a sentence or so. Do not compliment the board on the thoroughness of their examination – they have been sketchy, and you know it. If you wish, merely say, "No thank you, I have nothing further to add." This is a point where you can "talk yourself out" of a good impression or fail to present an important bit of information. Remember, *you close the interview yourself*.

The chairman will then say, "That is all, Mr. _____, thank you." Do not be startled; the interview is over, and quicker than you think. Thank him, gather your belongings and take your leave. Save your sigh of relief for the other side of the door.

How to put your best foot forward

Throughout this entire process, you may feel that the board individually and collectively is trying to pierce your defenses, seek out your hidden weaknesses and embarrass and confuse you. Actually, this is not true. They are obliged to make an appraisal of your qualifications for the job you are seeking, and they want to see you in your best light. Remember, they must interview all candidates and a non-cooperative candidate may become a failure in spite of their best efforts to bring out his qualifications. Here are 15 suggestions that will help you:

1) Be natural – Keep your attitude confident, not cocky

If you are not confident that you can do the job, do not expect the board to be. Do not apologize for your weaknesses, try to bring out your strong points. The board is interested in a positive, not negative, presentation. Cockiness will antagonize any board member and make him wonder if you are covering up a weakness by a false show of strength.

2) Get comfortable, but don't lounge or sprawl

Sit erectly but not stiffly. A careless posture may lead the board to conclude that you are careless in other things, or at least that you are not impressed by the importance of the occasion. Either conclusion is natural, even if incorrect. Do not fuss with your clothing, a pencil or an ashtray. Your hands may occasionally be useful to emphasize a point; do not let them become a point of distraction.

3) Do not wisecrack or make small talk

This is a serious situation, and your attitude should show that you consider it as such. Further, the time of the board is limited – they do not want to waste it, and neither should you.

4) Do not exaggerate your experience or abilities

In the first place, from information in the application or other interviews and sources, the board may know more about you than you think. Secondly, you probably will not get away with it. An experienced board is rather adept at spotting such a situation, so do not take the chance.

5) If you know a board member, do not make a point of it, yet do not hide it

Certainly you are not fooling him, and probably not the other members of the board. Do not try to take advantage of your acquaintanceship – it will probably do you little good.

6) Do not dominate the interview

Let the board do that. They will give you the clues – do not assume that you have to do all the talking. Realize that the board has a number of questions to ask you, and do not try to take up all the interview time by showing off your extensive knowledge of the answer to the first one.

7) Be attentive

You only have 20 minutes or so, and you should keep your attention at its sharpest throughout. When a member is addressing a problem or question to you, give him your undivided attention. Address your reply principally to him, but do not exclude the other board members.

8) Do not interrupt

A board member may be stating a problem for you to analyze. He will ask you a question when the time comes. Let him state the problem, and wait for the question.

9) Make sure you understand the question

Do not try to answer until you are sure what the question is. If it is not clear, restate it in your own words or ask the board member to clarify it for you. However, do not haggle about minor elements.

10) Reply promptly but not hastily

A common entry on oral board rating sheets is "candidate responded readily," or "candidate hesitated in replies." Respond as promptly and quickly as you can, but do not jump to a hasty, ill-considered answer.

11) Do not be peremptory in your answers

A brief answer is proper – but do not fire your answer back. That is a losing game from your point of view. The board member can probably ask questions much faster than you can answer them.

12) Do not try to create the answer you think the board member wants

He is interested in what kind of mind you have and how it works – not in playing games. Furthermore, he can usually spot this practice and will actually grade you down on it.

13) Do not switch sides in your reply merely to agree with a board member

Frequently, a member will take a contrary position merely to draw you out and to see if you are willing and able to defend your point of view. Do not start a debate, yet do not surrender a good position. If a position is worth taking, it is worth defending.

14) Do not be afraid to admit an error in judgment if you are shown to be wrong

The board knows that you are forced to reply without any opportunity for careful consideration. Your answer may be demonstrably wrong. If so, admit it and get on with the interview.

15) Do not dwell at length on your present job

The opening question may relate to your present assignment. Answer the question but do not go into an extended discussion. You are being examined for a *new* job, not your present one. As a matter of fact, try to phrase ALL your answers in terms of the job for which you are being examined.

Basis of Rating

Probably you will forget most of these "do's" and "don'ts" when you walk into the oral interview room. Even remembering them all will not ensure you a passing grade. Perhaps you did not have the qualifications in the first place. But remembering them will help you to put your best foot forward, without treading on the toes of the board members.

Rumor and popular opinion to the contrary notwithstanding, an oral board wants you to make the best appearance possible. They know you are under pressure – but they also want to see how you respond to it as a guide to what your reaction would be under the pressures of the job you seek. They will be influenced by the degree of poise you display, the personal traits you show and the manner in which you respond.

ABOUT THIS BOOK

This book contains tests divided into Examination Sections. Go through each test, answering every question in the margin. We have also attached a sample answer sheet at the back of the book that can be removed and used. At the end of each test look at the answer key and check your answers. On the ones you got wrong, look at the right answer choice and learn. Do not fill in the answers first. Do not memorize the questions and answers, but understand the answer and principles involved. On your test, the questions will likely be different from the samples. Questions are changed and new ones added. If you understand these past questions you should have success with any changes that arise. Tests may consist of several types of questions. We have additional books on each subject should more study be advisable or necessary for you. Finally, the more you study, the better prepared you will be. This book is intended to be the last thing you study before you walk into the examination room. Prior study of relevant texts is also recommended. NLC publishes some of these in our Fundamental Series. Knowledge and good sense are important factors in passing your exam. Good luck also helps. So now study this Passbook, absorb the material contained within and take that knowledge into the examination. Then do your best to pass that exam.

EXAMINATION SECTION

EXAMINATION SECTION
TEST 1

DIRECTIONS: Each question or incomplete statement is followed by several suggested answers or completions. Select the one that BEST answers the question or completes the statement. *PRINT THE LETTER OF THE CORRECT ANSWER IN THE SPACE AT THE RIGHT.*

Questions 1-8.

DIRECTIONS: Questions 1 through 8 are to be answered SOLELY on the basis of the following Memory Scene 1. Study this scene carefully for five minutes. Then answer Questions 1 through 8. Do not refer back to this scene when answering the questions.

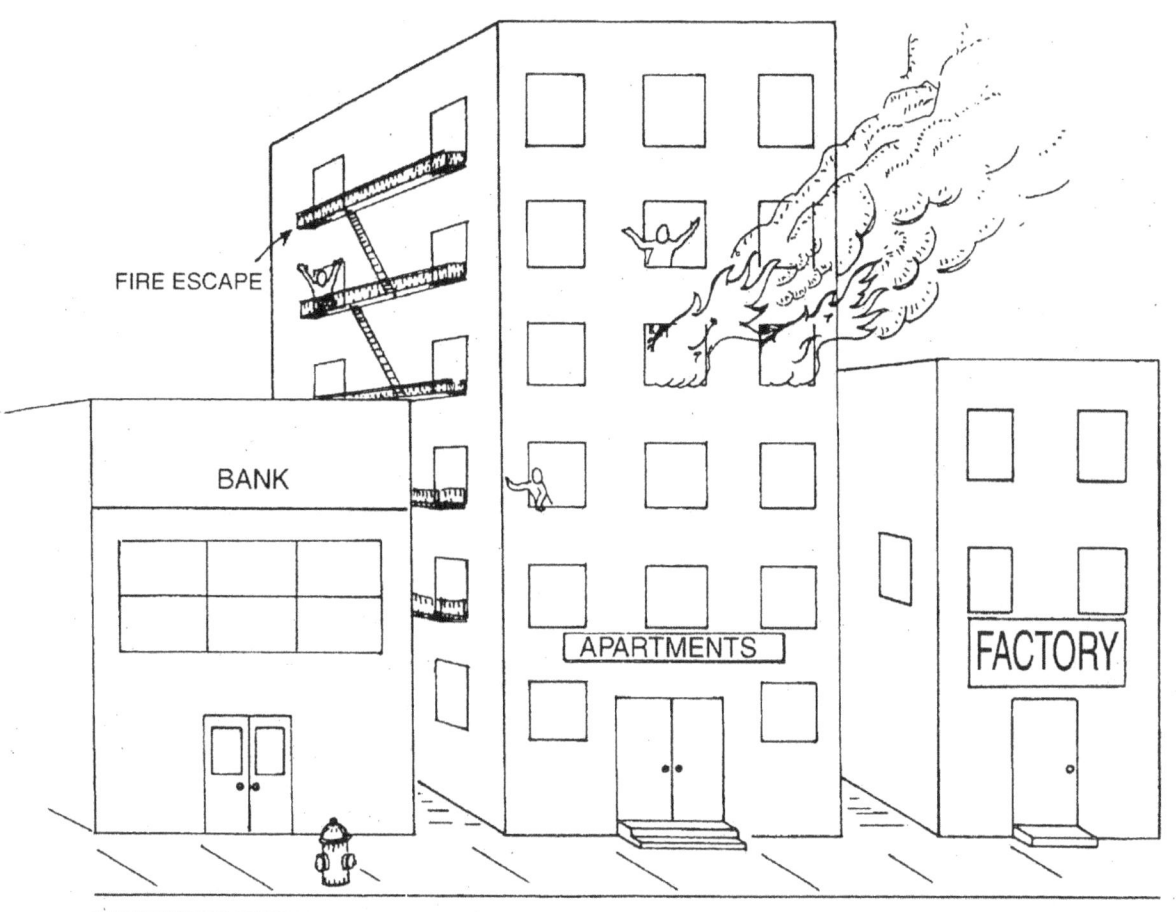

NOTE: THE GROUND FLOOR IS THE FIRST FLOOR

1. The fire is located on the _____ floor.

    A. first　　　　　B. fourth　　　　　C. fifth　　　　　D. top

1._____

2. The smoke and flames are blowing _____ and to the _____. 2._____

   A. up; left B. up; right
   C. down; left D. down; right

3. There is a person on a fire escape on the _____ floor. 3._____

   A. second B. third C. fourth D. fifth

4. Persons are visible in windows at the front of the building on fire on the _____ floors. 4._____

   A. second and third B. third and fifth
   C. fourth and sixth D. fifth and sixth

5. The person who is CLOSEST to the flames is in a _____ window on the _____ floor. 5._____

   A. front; third B. front; fifth
   C. side; fifth D. side; third

6. A firefighter is told to go to the roof of the building on fire. 6._____
   It would be CORRECT to state that the firefighter can cross directly to the roof from

   A. the roof of the bank
   B. the roof of the factory
   C. either the bank or the factory
   D. neither the bank nor the factory

7. On which side of the building on fire are fire escapes visible? 7._____

   A. Left B. Front C. Right D. Rear

8. The hydrant on the sidewalk is 8._____

   A. in front of the bank
   B. between the bank and the apartments
   C. in front of the apartments
   D. between the apartments and the factory

Questions 9-16.

DIRECTIONS: Questions 9 through 16 are to be answered on the basis of the following floor plan.
Look at this floor plan of an apartment. It is on the 3rd floor of the building. The floor plan also indicates the public hallway.

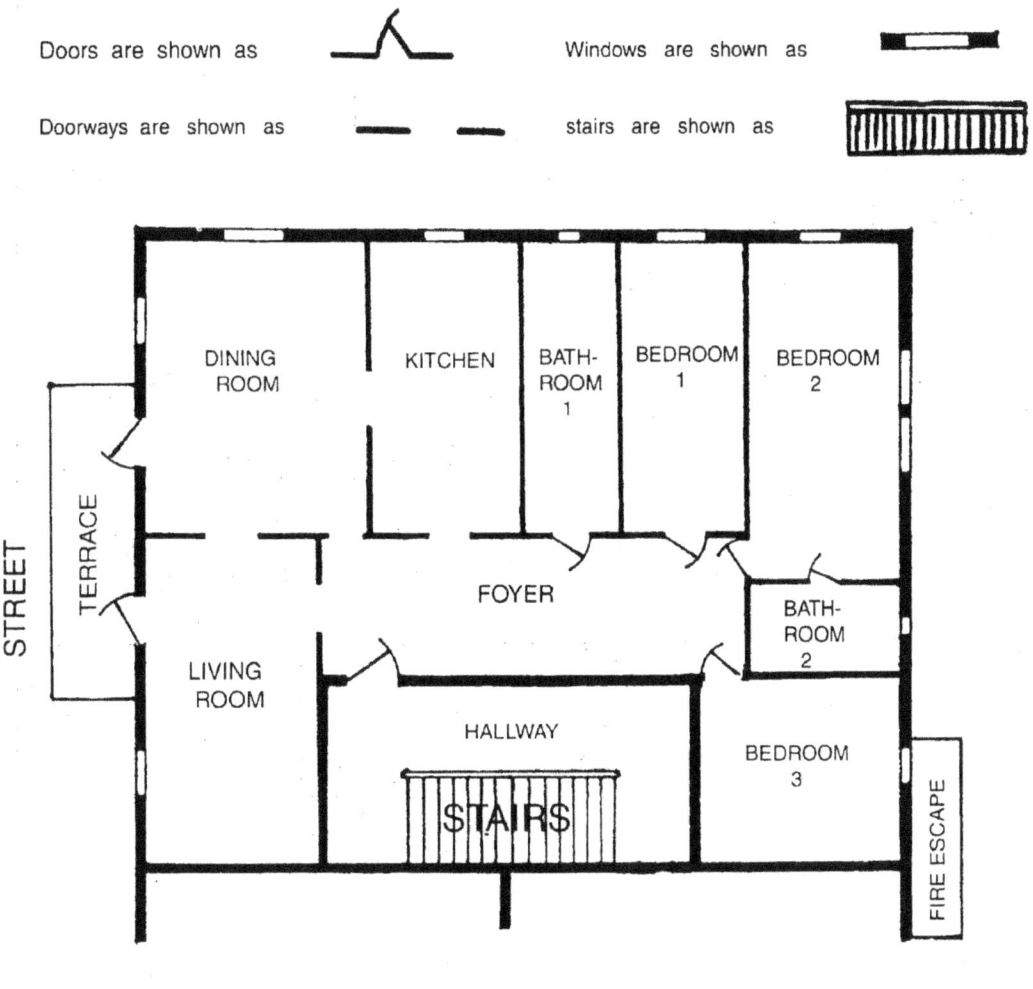

9. Which room is FARTHEST from the fire escape?

    A. Bedroom 2
    B. Bedroom 3
    C. Kitchen
    D. Dining room

10. Which one of the following rooms has ONLY one door or doorway?

    A. Living room
    B. Bedroom 1
    C. Kitchen
    D. Dining room

11. Which room can firefighters reach DIRECTLY from the fire escape?

    A. Dining room
    B. Living room
    C. Bedroom 1
    D. Bedroom 3

12. Which room does NOT have a door or doorway leading directly to the foyer?

    A. Bathroom 1
    B. Bathroom 2
    C. Bedroom 1
    D. Dining room

13. A firefighter leaving Bathroom 2 would be in

    A. bedroom 1
    B. bedroom 2
    C. bedroom 3
    D. the foyer

14. Firefighters on the terrace would be able to enter directly into which rooms?

    A. Bedroom 1 and bathroom 1
    B. Bedroom 2 and bathroom 2
    C. Dining room and kitchen
    D. Dining room and living room

15. Which rooms have AT LEAST one window on two sides of the building?

    A. Bedroom 2 and dining room
    B. Bedroom 2 and bedroom 3
    C. Dining room and living room
    D. Dining room, bedroom 2, and bedroom 3

16. Firefighters can enter the kitchen directly from the foyer and

    A. bedroom 1   B. the living room
    C. bathroom 1   D. the dining room

17. Firefighters are often required to rescue individuals from a fire. The GREATEST possibility of a firefighter having to rescue someone in a private home occurs between the hours of

    A. 7 A.M. and 11 A.M.   B. 10 A.M. and 2 P.M.
    C. 2 P.M. and 6 P.M.   D. 2 A.M. and 6 A.M.

18. At a fire in an apartment building, a firefighter is told to inform the lieutenant if she finds any dangerous conditions in the basement.
    Which one of the following is the MOST dangerous condition?

    A. Gas is leaking from a broken pipe.
    B. The sewer pipe is broken.
    C. Water is seeping into the basement.
    D. The electricity has been turned off.

19. Firefighters are required to use portable ladders to rescue people.
    When firefighters are positioning a portable ladder for a rescue, which one of the following would present the GREATEST threat to the firefighters' safety?

    A. A person to be rescued who is standing near an open window
    B. Tree branches which are close to the ladder
    C. A person to be rescued who is dressed in a long robe
    D. Overhead electrical wires which are close to the ladder

20. Firefighters are instructed to notify an officer whenever they attempt to rescue someone who is seriously endangered by fire or smoke. Firefighters respond to a fire in a 6-story apartment building. The fire is in a fourth floor apartment in the front of the building. Firefighters should notify an officer when they are attempting to rescue

    A. a person who disappears from a smoke-filled window on the fourth floor
    B. a person who is on the roof
    C. three persons on the third floor rear fire escape who appear to be very frightened
    D. two children who are locked in their apartment on the first floor

21. Firefighters who forcibly enter an apartment on fire may find conditions which indicate that they should immediately search for victims.
Of the following conditions in an apartment on fire, which one would MOST clearly indicate to firefighters that they should immediately search for victims?

    A. There is a pot on the stove.
    B. The apartment door was chain-locked from the inside.
    C. Water is dripping into a pail.
    D. All the windows in the apartment are closed.

21._____

Questions 22-24.

DIRECTIONS: Questions 22 through 24 are to be answered SOLELY on the basis of the following passage.

When there is a fire in a subway train, it may be necessary for firefighters to evacuate people from the trains by way of the tunnels. In every tunnel, there are emergency exit areas which have stairways that can be used to evacuate people to the street from the track area. All emergency exits can be recognized by an exit sign near a group of five white lights.

There is a Blue Light Area which is located every 600 feet in the tunnel. These areas contain a power removal box, a telephone, and a fire extinguisher. Removal of power from the third rail is the first step firefighters must take when evacuating people through tunnels. When a firefighter uses the power removal box to turn off electrical power during evacuation procedures, the firefighter must immediately telephone the trainmaster and explain the reason for the power removal. Communication between the firefighter and the trainmaster is essential. If the trainmaster does not receive a phone call within four minutes after power removal, the power will be restored to the third rail.

22. When evacuating passengers through the subway tunnel, firefighters must FIRST

    A. telephone the trainmaster for assistance
    B. remove electrical power from the third rail
    C. locate the emergency exit in the tunnel
    D. go to the group of five white lights

22._____

23. Immediately after using the power removal box to turn off the electrical power, a firefighter should

    A. wait four minutes before calling the trainmaster
    B. begin evacuating passengers through the tunnel
    C. call the trainmaster and explain why the power was turned off
    D. touch the third rail to see if the electrical power has been turned off

23._____

24. A group of five white lights in a subway tunnel indicates that

    A. a telephone is available
    B. the electrical power is off in the third rail
    C. a fire extinguisher is available
    D. an emergency exit is located there

24._____

25. During a recent day tour with an engine company, Firefighter Sims was assigned to the control position on the hose. The company responded to the following alarms during this tour:

Alarm 1: At 9:30 A.M., the company responded to a fire on the first floor of an apartment building. At the fire scene, Firefighter Sims pulled the hose from the fire engine and assisted the driver in attaching the hose to the hydrant.

Alarm 2: At 11:00 A.M., the company responded to a fire on the third floor of a vacant building. Firefighter Sims pulled the hose from the fire engine and went to the building on fire.

Alarm 3: At 1:00 P.M., the company responded to a fire in a first-floor laundromat. Firefighter Sims pulled the hose from the fire engine and assisted the driver in attaching the hose to the hydrant.

Alarm 4: At 3:00 P.M., the company responded to a fire on the fourth floor of an apartment building. Firefighter Sims pulled the hose from the fire engine and went to the building on fire.

Alarm 5: At 5:45 P.M., the company responded to a fire on the second floor of a private house. Firefighter Sims pulled the hose from the fire engine and assisted the driver in attaching the hose to the hydrant.

The firefighter assigned to the control position assists the driver in attaching the hose to a hydrant when the fire is

A. in an apartment building
B. above the second floor
C. in a vacant building
D. below the third floor

KEY (CORRECT ANSWERS)

1. B
2. B
3. D
4. B
5. B
6. D
7. A
8. A
9. D
10. B
11. D
12. B
13. B
14. D
15. A
16. D
17. D
18. A
19. D
20. A
21. B
22. B
23. C
24. D
25. D

TEST 2

DIRECTIONS: Each question or incomplete statement is followed by several suggested answers or completions. Select the one that BEST answers the question or completes the statement. *PRINT THE LETTER OF THE CORRECT ANSWER IN THE SPACE AT THE RIGHT.*

Questions 1-3.

DIRECTIONS: Questions 1 through 3 are to be answered on the basis of the following floor plan and the paragraph which appears on the next page.

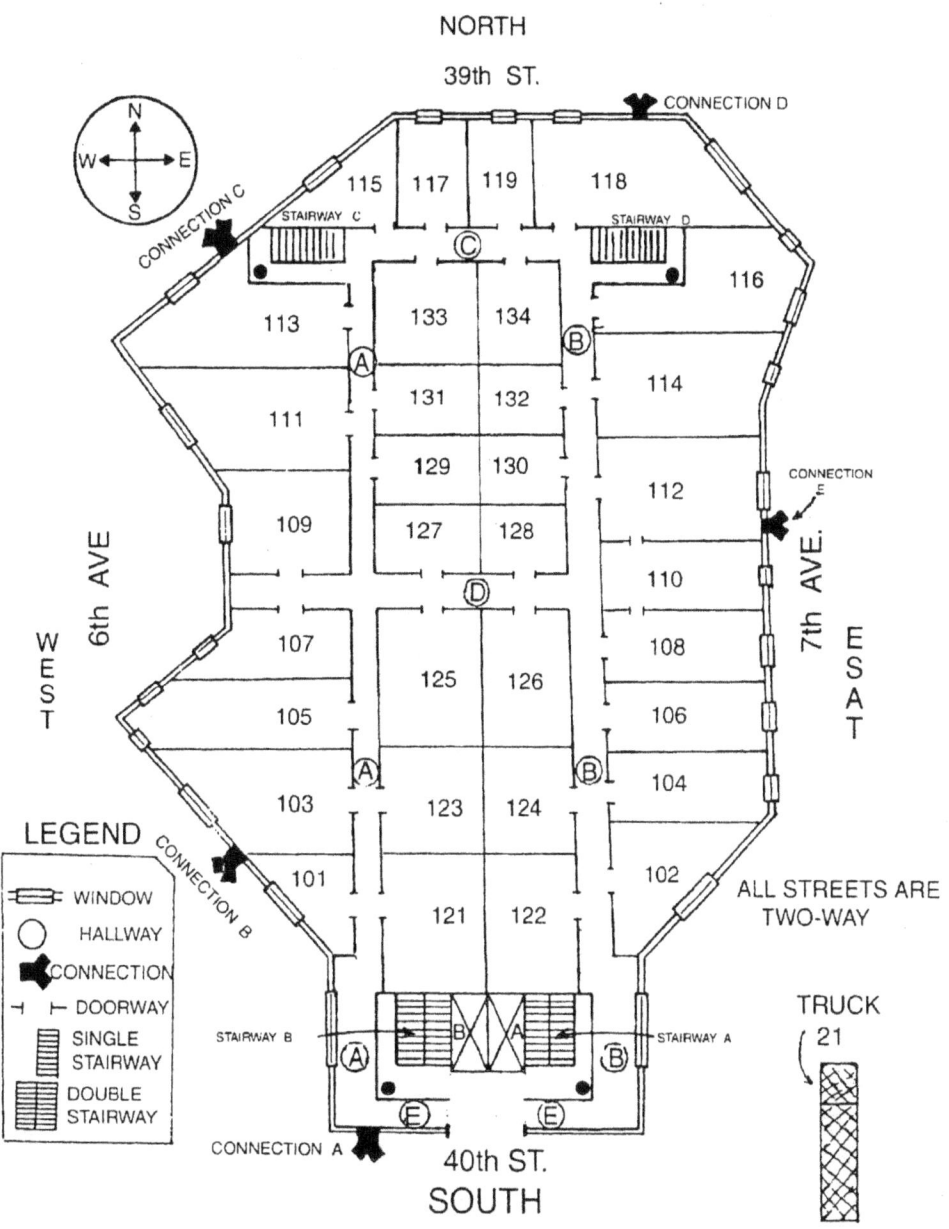

The floor plan represents a typical high-rise office building in midtown. Numbers shown indicate room numbers. The pipe connections for the water supply system are outside the building at street level. Firefighters attach hoses to those connections to send water into the pipes in the building.

7

Questions 1 through 3 refer to a fire on the 1st floor in Room 111.

1. After fighting the fire in Room 111, firefighters are instructed to go immediately to the east-west hallway in the center of the building and search for victims in that hallway. Which one of the following lists ALL of the rooms that the firefighters should search?

    A. 115, 117, 118, 119, 133, and 134
    B. 125, 126, 127, 128, and 129
    C. 107, 109, 125, 126, 127, and 128
    D. 121, 122, 123, 124, 125, and 126

2. Firefighters are told to search Room 134. They enter the building from 40th Street. What is the SHORTEST route for the firefighters to take to reach this room?

    A. West in hallway E, north in hallway A, then east in hallway C
    B. West in hallway E, north in hallway A, east in hallway D, north in hallway B, then west in hallway C
    C. East in hallway E, north in hallway B, then west in hallway C
    D. East in hallway E, north in hallway B, west in hallway D, north in hallway A, then east in hallway C

3. Firefighters in Truck 21 have been ordered to attach a hose to a connection outside the building. The fire-fighters cannot use connection A because 40th Street is blocked by traffic.
   What is the FIRST connection the firefighters can drive to? Connection

    A. B   B. C   C. D   D. E

Questions 4-6.

DIRECTIONS: Questions 4 through 6 are to be answered on the basis of the following passage.

Firefighters often know the appearance and construction features of apartments by recognizing the general features on the outside of the building. The following are some general features of different types of buildings in the city.

   1. OLD LAW TENEMENTS:
      Height - 5 to 7 stories
      Width - 25 feet
      Fire Escapes - There will be a rear fire escape if there are two apartments per floor. There will be front and rear fire escapes if there are four apartments per floor.
   2. ROW FRAMES:
      Height - 2 to 5 stories
      Width - 20 feet to 30 feet
      Fire Escapes - There will be a rear fire escape if the building is higher than 2 stories.
   3. BROWNSTONES:
      Height - 3 to 5 stories
      Width - 20 feet to 25 feet
      Fire Escapes - If the brownstone has been changed from a private home to a multiple dwelling, there will be a rear fire escape. Unchanged brownstones have no fire escapes.

4. Upon arrival at a fire, a firefighter observes that the building is 3 stories high and 25 feet wide. There are fire escapes only in the rear of the building.
   The firefighter should conclude that the building is either a

   A. Row Frame or an unchanged Brownstone
   B. Row Frame or an Old Law Tenement with two apartments per floor
   C. changed Brownstone or an Old Law Tenement with four apartments per floor
   D. Row Frame or a changed Brownstone

4._____

5. At another fire, the building is 5 stories high and 25 feet wide. There is a front fire escape.
   The firefighters should conclude that this building has

   A. a rear fire escape because the building is a Row Frame higher than two stories
   B. a rear fire escape because the building is an Old Law Tenement with four apartments per floor
   C. no rear fire escape because the building is a Brown-stone that has been changed into a multiple dwelling
   D. no rear fire escape because the building has a front fire escape

5._____

6. At another fire, the building is 4 stories high and 30 feet wide. The building has no front fire escape.
   The firefighter should conclude that the building is a(n)

   A. Row Frame which has no rear fire escape
   B. Old Law Tenement which has four apartments per floor
   C. Row Frame which has a rear fire escape
   D. Brownstone which has been changed from a private home to a multiple dwelling

6._____

Questions 7-9.

DIRECTIONS: Questions 7 through 9 are to be answered on the basis of the following passage.

Firefighters use 2-way radios to alert other firefighters of dangerous conditions and of the need for help. Messages should begin with *MAY DAY* or *URGENT*. *MAY DAY* messages have priority over *URGENT* messages. Following is a list of specific emergencies and the messages which should be sent.

MAY DAY Messages:

1. When a collapse is probable in the area where the firefighters are working: *MAY DAY - MAY DAY, collapse probable, GET OUT.*
2. When a collapse has occurred in the area where the firefighters are working: *MAY DAY - MAY DAY, collapse occurred.* The firefighter should also give the location of the collapse. If there are trapped victims, the number and condition of the trapped victims is also given.
3. When a firefighter appears to be a heart attack victim: *MAY DAY- MAY DAY, CARDIAC.* The location of the victim is also given.
4. When anyone has a serious, life-threatening injury: *MAY DAY - MAY DAY.* The firefighter also describes the injury and gives the condition and the location of the victim.

Messages:

1. When anyone has a less serious injury which requires medical attention (for example, a broken arm): *URGENT - URGENT.* The firefighter also gives the type of injury and the location of the victim.
2. When the firefighters should leave the building and fight the fire from the outside: *URGENT - URGENT, back out.* The firefighter also indicates the area to be evacuated.
3. *URGENT* messages should also be sent when firefighters' lives are endangered due to a drastic loss of water pressure in the hose.

7. Firefighters are ordered to extinguish a fire on the third floor of an apartment building. As the firefighters are operating the hose on the third floor, the stairway collapses and cuts the hose.
   What message should the firefighters send?

   A. URGENT - URGENT, back out
   B. URGENT - URGENT, we have a loss of water on the third floor
   C. MAY DAY - MAY DAY, collapse occurred on third floor stairway
   D. MAY DAY - MAY DAY, collapse probable, GET OUT

8. Two firefighters on the second floor of a vacant building are discussing the possibility of the floor's collapse. One of the firefighters clutches his chest and falls down. What message should the other firefighter send?

   A. MAY DAY - MAY DAY, firefighter collapse on the second floor
   B. MAY DAY - MAY DAY, CARDIAC on the second floor
   C. URGENT - URGENT, firefighter unconscious on the second floor
   D. URGENT - URGENT, collapse probable on the second floor

9. A firefighter has just decided that a collapse of the third floor is probable when he falls and breaks his wrist.
   What is the FIRST message he should send?

   A. URGENT - URGENT, broken wrist on the third floor
   B. MAY DAY - MAY DAY, broken wrist on the third floor
   C. MAY DAY - MAY DAY, collapse probable, GET OUT
   D. URGENT - URGENT, back out, third floor

Questions 10-11.

DIRECTIONS: Questions 10 and 11 are to be answered on the basis of the following information and the diagram which appears on the next page.

An 8-story apartment building has scissor stairs beginning on the first floor and going to the roof. Scissor stairs are two separate stairways (Stairway A and Stairway B) that crisscross each other and lead to opposite sides of the building on each floor. Once a person has entered either stairway, the only way to cross over to the other stairway on any floor is by leaving the stairway and using the hallway on that floor. A person entering Stairway A, which starts on the east side of the building on the first floor, would end up on the west side of the building on the second floor, and back on the east side on the third floor. Similarly, a person entering Stairway B, which starts on the west side of the building on the first floor, would end up on the east side of the building on the second floor, and back on the west side on the third floor.

The apartment building has one water pipe for fighting fires. This pipe runs in a straight line near the stairway on the east side of the building from the first floor to the roof. There are water outlets for this pipe on each floor.

Both of the following questions involve a fire in an apartment on the west side of the 6th floor.

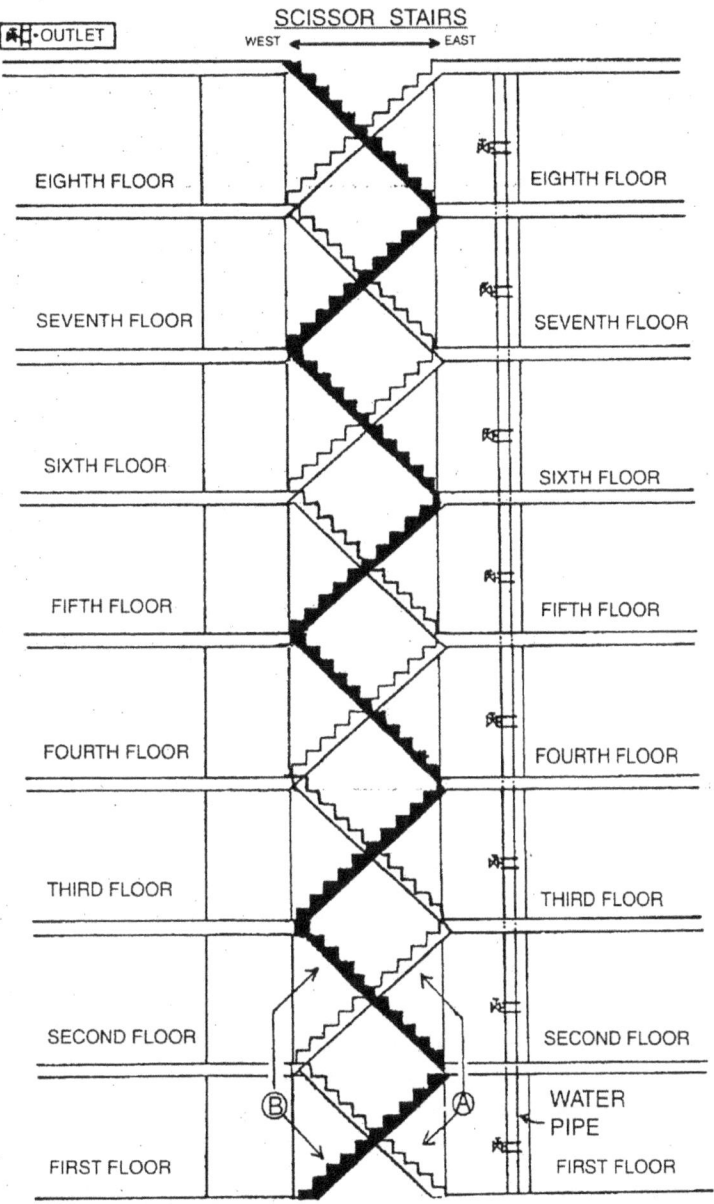

10. Firefighters are ordered to connect a hose to the nearest outlet below the fire. Upon reaching this outlet, they find that it is not usable.
Where is the next available outlet?
_____ floor near Stairway _____.

   A. 5th; B   B. 3rd; A   C. 4th; B   D. 4th; A

11. A firefighter working on the west side of the 7th floor is ordered to search for victims on the west side of the 8th floor. The door leading to the stairway on the west side of the 7th floor is jammed shut.
To reach the victims, the firefighter should take

   A. Stairway A to the 8th floor, and then go across the hallway to the west side of the floor
   B. Stairway B to the 8th floor, and then go across the hallway to the west side of the floor
   C. the hallway to the east side of the 7th floor and go up Stairway A
   D. the hallway to the east side of the 7th floor and go up Stairway B

12. Firefighters refer to the four sides of a building on fire as *exposures*. The front of the fire building is referred to as Exposure 1. Exposures 2, 3, and 4 follow in clock wise order. Firefighters are working at a building whose front entrance faces south. A firefighter who is in the center of the roof is ordered to go to Exposure 3.
To reach Exposure 3, the direction in which he must walk is

   A. east   B. west   C. south   D. north

Questions 13-17.

DIRECTIONS: Questions 13 through 17 are to be answered SOLELY on the basis of the following passage.

The most important activities which firefighters perform at fires are search, rescue, ventilation, and extinguishment. Ventilation is a vital part of firefighting because it prevents fire from spreading to other areas and because it enables firefighters to search for victims and to bring hoses closer to the fire area. Two types of ventilation used by firefighters are natural venting and mechanical venting. Both types permit the vertical and horizontal movement of smoke and gas from a fire building.

Natural vertical ventilation is generally performed on the roof of the building on fire by making an opening. This allows the heat and smoke to travel up and out of the fire building. Opening windows in the fire area is an example of natural horizontal ventilation. This allows the heat and smoke to travel out of the windows.

Mechanical ventilation takes place when mechanical devices, such as smoke ejectors or hoses with nozzles, are used to remove heated gases from an area. A smoke ejector might be used in a cellar fire when smoke has traveled to the far end of the cellar, creating a heavy smoke condition that cannot be removed naturally. The smoke ejector would be brought into the area to draw the smoke out of the cellar. A nozzle is used with a hose to create a fine spray of water. When directed towards an open window, the water spray pushes smoke and heated gases out of the window.

Extinguishment means bringing a hose to the fire and operating the nozzle to put water on the fire. The proper positioning of hoses is essential to firefighting tactics. Most lives are saved at fires by the proper positioning of hoses.

At each fire, firefighters must use the quickest and best method of extinguishment. There are times when an immediate and direct attack on the fire is required. This means that the hose is brought directly to the fire itself. A fire in a vacant lot, or a fire in the entrance of a building, calls for an immediate and direct attack on the fire.

It is generally the ladder company that is assigned the tasks of venting, search, and rescue while the engine company performs the task of extinguishment.

13. Ventilation performed at the roof is GENERALLY _____ ventilation.

    A. mechanical vertical
    B. natural vertical
    C. natural horizontal
    D. mechanical horizontal

14. When an immediate and direct attack on the fire is required, the hose is

    A. positioned between the building on fire and the building which the fire might spread to
    B. brought to a window in order to push smoke and gases out
    C. brought to the roof to push the smoke and gases out
    D. brought directly to the fire itself

15. Ladder companies are GENERALLY assigned the tasks of

    A. extinguishment, rescue, and search
    B. extinguishment, venting, and search
    C. venting, search, and rescue
    D. venting, rescue, and extinguishment

16. MOST lives are saved at fires by

    A. a systematic search
    B. the proper positioning of hoses
    C. the proper performance of ventilation
    D. the use of nozzles for ventilation and extinguishment

17. Ventilation enables firefighters to

    A. bring hoses to the fire and search for victims
    B. create a fine spray of water
    C. use a nozzle to remove smoke and gases
    D. use an ejector to draw smoke out of an area

Questions 18-19.

DIRECTIONS: Questions 18 and 19 are to be answered SOLELY on the basis of the following passage.

A new firefighter learns the following facts about his company's response area: All the factories are located between 9th Avenue and 12th Avenue, from 42nd Street to 51st Street; all the apartment buildings are located between 7th Avenue and 9th Avenue, from 47th Street to 51st Street; all the private houses are located between 5th Avenue and 9th Avenue, from 42nd. Street to 47th Street; and all the stores are located between 5th Avenue and 7th Avenue, from 47th Street to 51st Street.

The firefighter also learns that the apartment buildings are all between 4 and 6 stories; the private houses are all between 1 and 3 stories; the factories are all between 3 and 5 stories; and the stores are all either 1 or 2 stories.

18. An alarm is received for a fire located on 8th Avenue between 46th Street and 47th Street.
A firefighter should assume that the fire is in a

   A. private house between 1 and 3 stories
   B. private house between 4 and 6 stories
   C. factory between 3 and 5 stories
   D. factory between 4 and 6 stories

19. The company responds to a fire on 47th Street between 6th Avenue and 7th Avenue. The firefighter should assume that he would be responding to a fire in a(n)

   A. store of either 1 or 2 stories
   B. factory between 3 and 5 stories
   C. apartment building between 4 and 6 stories
   D. private house between 4 and 6 stories

Questions 20-25.

DIRECTIONS: Questions 20 through 25 are to be answered on the basis of the following information and the diagram which appears on the next page.

At three o'clock in the morning, a fire alarm is received for the area shown in the diagram. A train loaded with highly flammable material is on fire. The entire area is surrounded by a ten-foot-high fence. At the time of the fire, Gate A is open and Gates B, C, and D are locked.

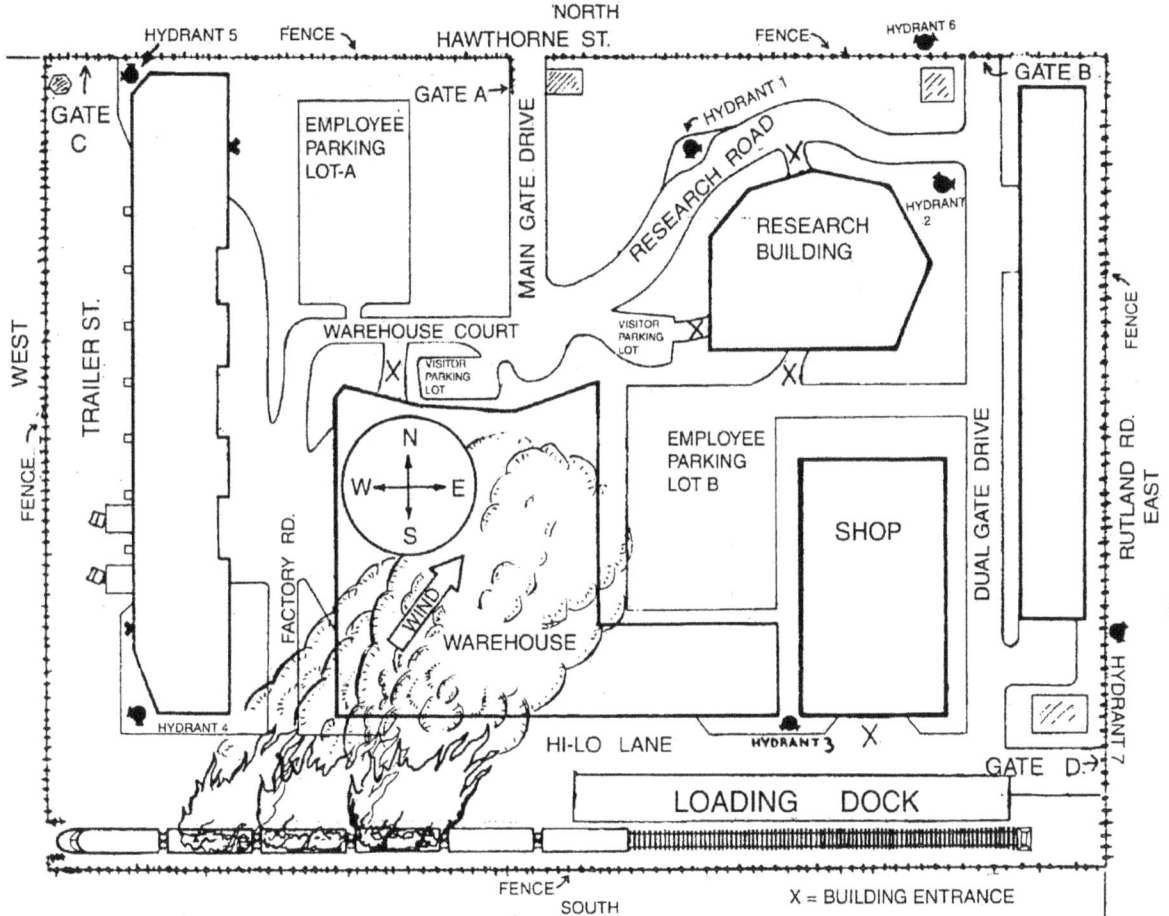

20. The first engine company arrives at the fire scene. The security guard at Gate A informs the firefighters of the location of the fire. Firefighter Jensen knows the area. He should inform the lieutenant that the way to drive to a hydrant that is as close to the fire as possible without passing through the smoke and flames is by going

    A. south on Main Gate Drive, east on Research Road, south on Dual Gate Drive, and west on Hi-Lo Lane to hydrant 3
    B. south on Main Gate Drive, west on Warehouse Court, south on Factory Road, and west on Hi-Lo Lane to hydrant 4
    C. south on Main Gate Drive and east on Research Road to hydrant 1
    D. east on Hawthorne Street and south on Rutland Road to hydrant 7

21. Firefighters at Employee Parking Lot A are ordered to drive their truck to the fence outside Gate D.
    Which of the following is the SHORTEST route the fire-fighters could take from Warehouse Court?

    A. South on Factory Road, then west on Hi-Lo Lane, and north on Trailer Street
    B. East on Research Road, and south on Dual Gate Drive
    C. North on Main Gate Drive, east on Hawthorne Street, and south on Rutland Road
    D. North on Main Gate Drive, west on Hawthorne Street, south on Trailer Street, and west on Hi-Lo Lane

22. The first ladder company arrives at the fire scene. As they are driving north on Rutland Road, firefighters see the fire through Gate D. They cut the locks and enter Gate D. The lieutenant orders a firefighter to go on foot from Gate D to the Research Building and to search it for occupants.
The entrance to the Research Building which is CLOSEST to this firefighter is

    A. connected to the Visitor Parking Lot
    B. located on Research Road
    C. connected to Parking Lot B
    D. located on Dual Gate Drive

23. The second engine company to arrive is ordered to attach a hose to a hydrant located outside of the fenced area and then to await further orders.
The hydrant outside of the fenced area which is CLOSEST to the flames is hydrant

    A. 6   B. 3   C. 4   D. 7

24. The second ladder company to arrive at the fire scene is met at Gate C by a security guard who gives them the keys to open all the gates. They drive south on Trailer Street to the corner of Hi-Lo Lane and Trailer Street. The company is then ordered to drive to the corner of Research Road and Dual Gate Drive.
Which is the SHORTEST route for the company to take with-out being exposed to the smoke and flames?

    A. East on Hi-Lo Lane, north on Factory Road, and east on Warehouse Court to Research Road
    B. East on Hi-Lo Lane and north on Dual Gate Drive
    C. North on Trailer Street, east on Hawthorne Street, and south on Dual Gate Drive
    D. North on Trailer Street, east on Hawthorne Street, south on Main Gate Drive, and east on Research Road

25. The heat from the fire in the railroad cars ignites the warehouse on the other side of Hi-Lo Lane. The officer of the first ladder company orders two firefighters who are on the west end of the loading dock to break the windows on the north side of the warehouse.
Of the following, the SHORTEST way for the firefighters to reach the northwest corner of the warehouse without passing through the smoke and flames is to go

    A. east on Hi-Lo Lane, north on Dual Gate Drive, and then west on Research Road to the entrance on Warehouse Court
    B. west on Hi-Lo Lane, north on Factory Road, and then east on Warehouse Court to the Visitor Parking Lot on Warehouse Court
    C. east on Hi-Lo Lane, north on Rutland Road, west on Hawthorne Street, and then south on Main Gate Drive to the Visitor Parking Lot on Warehouse Court
    D. east on Hi-Lo Lane, north on Dual Gate Drive, west on Hawthorne Street, and then south on Main Gate Drive to the entrance on Warehouse Court

KEY (CORRECT ANSWERS)

1. C
2. C
3. D
4. D
5. B

6. C
7. C
8. B
9. C
10. C

11. C
12. D
13. B
14. D
15. C

16. B
17. A
18. A
19. A
20. A

21. C
22. C
23. D
24. C
25. A

EXAMINATION SECTION
TEST 1

DIRECTIONS: Each question or incomplete statement is followed by several suggested answers or completions. Select the one that BEST answers the question or completes the statement. *PRINT THE LETTER OF THE CORRECT ANSWER IN THE SPACE AT THE RIGHT.*

Questions 1-5.

DIRECTIONS: Questions 1 through 5 are to be answered SOLELY on the basis of the following information and map.

A firefighter may be required to assist civilians who seek travel directions or referral to city agencies and facilities.

The following is a map of part of a city, where several public offices and other institutions are located. Each of the squares represents one city block. Street names are as shown. If there is an arrow next to the street name, it means the street is one way only in the direction of the arrow. If there is no arrow next to the street name, two-way traffic is allowed.

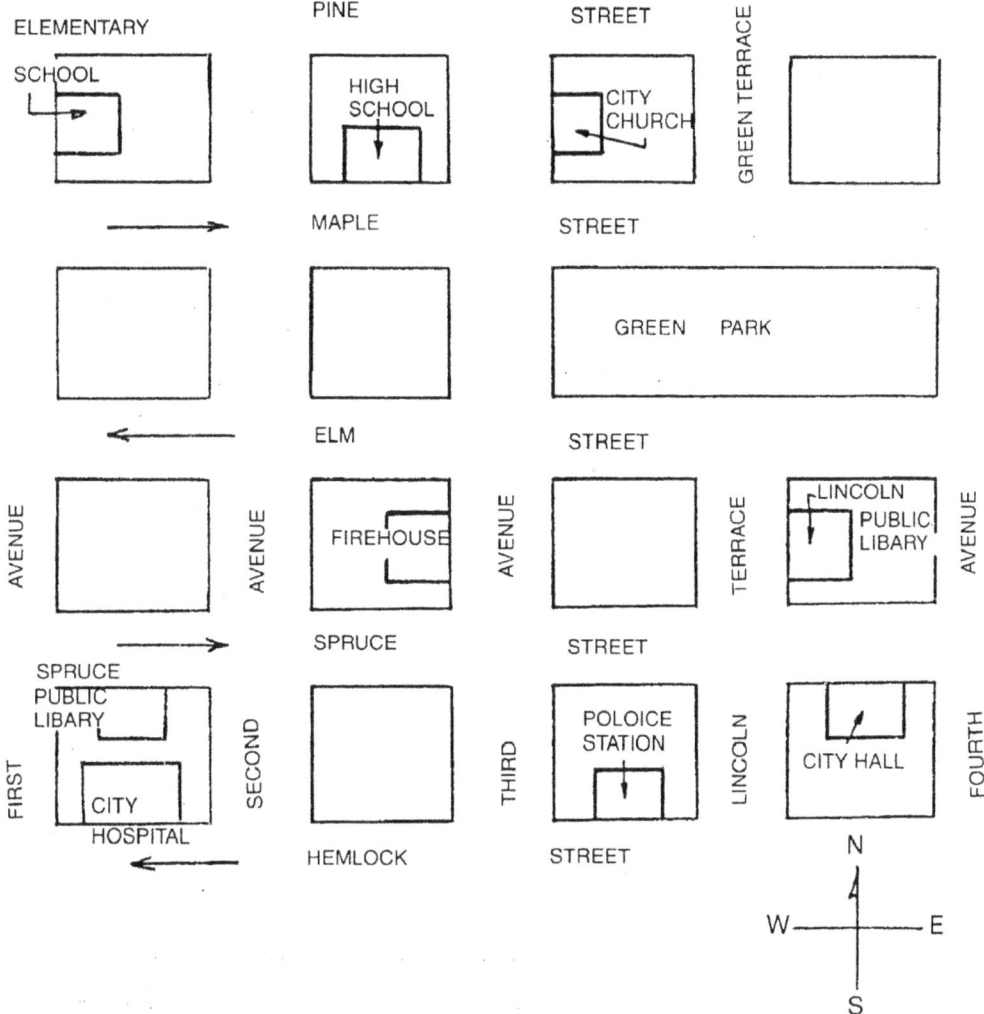

19

1. A woman whose handbag was stolen from her in Green Park asks a firefighter at the firehouse where to go to report the crime.
   The firefighter should tell the woman to go to the

   A. police station on Spruce St.
   B. police station on Hemlock St.
   C. city hall on Spruce St.
   D. city hall on Hemlock St.

2. A disabled senior citizen who lives on Green Terrace telephones the firehouse to ask which library is closest to her home.
   The firefighter should tell the senior citizen it is the

   A. Spruce Public Library on Lincoln Terrace
   B. Lincoln Public Library on Spruce Street
   C. Spruce Public Library on Spruce Street
   D. Lincoln Public Library on Lincoln Terrace

3. A woman calls the firehouse to ask for the exact location of City Hall.
   She should be told that it is on

   A. Hemlock Street, between Lincoln Terrace and Fourth Ave.
   B. Spruce Street, between Lincoln Terrace and Fourth Ave.
   C. Lincoln Terrace, between Spruce Street and Elm Street
   D. Green Terrace, between Maple Street and Pine Street

4. A delivery truck driver is having trouble finding the high school to make a delivery. The driver parks the truck across from the firehouse on Third Avenue facing north and goes into the firehouse to ask directions.
   In giving directions, the firefighter should tell the driver to go _____ to the school.

   A. north on Third Avenue to Pine Street and then make a right
   B. south on Third Avenue, make a left on Hemlock Street, and then make a right on Second Avenue
   C. north on Third Avenue, turn left on Elm Street, make a right on Second Avenue and go to Maple Street, then make another right
   D. north on Third Avenue to Maple Street, and then make a left

5. A man comes to the firehouse accompanied by his son and daughter. He wants to register his son in the high school and his daughter in the elementary school. He asks a firefighter which school is closest for him to walk to from the firehouse.
   The firefighter should tell the man that the

   A. high school is closer than the elementary school
   B. elementary school is closer than the high school
   C. elementary school and high school are the same distance away
   D. elementary school and the high school are in opposite directions

Questions 6-10.

DIRECTIONS: Questions 6 through 10 are to be answered SOLELY on the basis of the following passage.

Sometimes a fire engine leaving the scene of a fire must back out of a street because other fire engines have blocked the path in front of it. When the fire engine is backing up, each firefighter is given a duty to perform to help control automobile traffic and protect people walking nearby. Before the driver starts to slowly back up the fire engine, all the other firefighters are told the route he will take. They walk alongside and behind the slowly moving fire engine, guiding the driver, keeping traffic out of the street and warning people away from the path of the vehicle. As the fire engine, in reverse gear, approaches the intersection, the driver brings it to a full stop and waits for his supervisor to give the order to start moving again. If traffic is blocking the intersection, two firefighters enter the intersection to direct traffic. They clear the cars and people out of the intersection, making way for the fire engine to back into it. The driver then goes forward, turning into the intersection. Two other firefighters keep cars and people away from the front of the fire engine as it moves. Because of the extra care needed to control cars and protect people in the streets when a fire engine is backing up, it is better to drive a fire engine forward whenever possible.

6. A fire engine is leaving the scene of a fire. The street in front of it is blocked by people and other fire engines. Of the following, it would be BEST for the driver to

   A. put on the siren to clear a path
   B. back out of the street slowly
   C. drive on the sidewalk around the other fire engines
   D. move the other fire engines out of the way

7. Firefighters walk alongside and behind the fire engine when it is backing up in order to

   A. strengthen their legs and stay physically fit
   B. look around the neighborhood for fires
   C. insure that the engine moves slowly
   D. control traffic, protect people, and assist the driver

8. A fire engine going in reverse approaches an intersection blocked with cars and trucks. The driver should

   A. go forward and then try to back into the intersection at a different angle
   B. slowly enter the intersection as the firefighters guiding the driver give the signal to move
   C. back up through the intersection without stopping
   D. stop, then enter the intersection only when the supervisor gives the signal to move

9. The above passage states that the two firefighters who first enter the intersection

   A. clear the intersection of cars and people
   B. direct the cars past the fire engine when the engine is in forward gear
   C. see if the traffic signal is working properly
   D. set up barriers to block any traffic

10. The diagram to the right shows a fire engine backing slowly out of Jones Street. The letters indicate where firefighters are standing. Which firefighter is NOT in the correct position? Firefighter
   A. D
   B. E
   C. A
   D. C

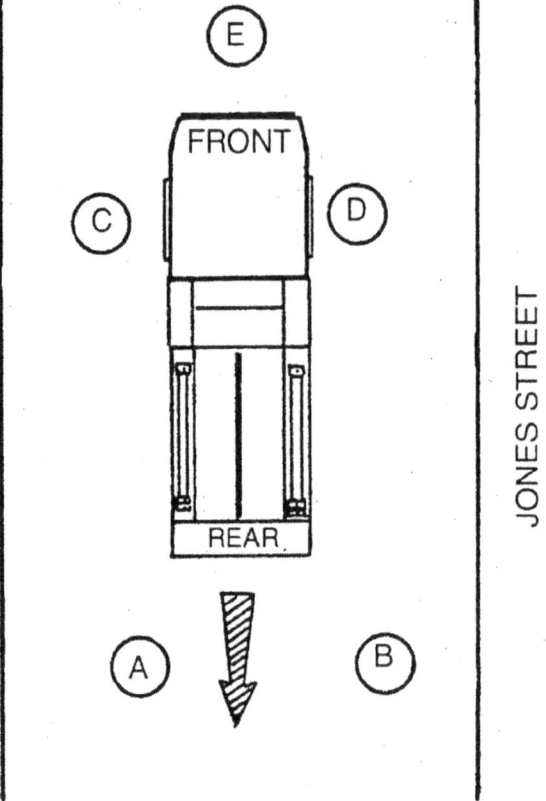

Questions 11-14.

DIRECTIONS: Questions 11 through 14 are to be answered SOLELY on the basis of the following passage.

    About 48% of all reported fires are false alarms. False alarms add more risk of danger to firefighters, citizens, and property as well as waste the money and time of the fire department. When the first firefighters are called to a reported fire, they do not know if the alarm is for a real fire or is a false alarm. Until they have made sure that the alarm is false, they must not respond to a new alarm even if a real fire is burning and people's lives and property are in danger. If they do not find a fire or an emergency at the original location, then the firefighters radio the fire department that they have been called to a false alarm. The fire department radios back and tells the firefighters that they are in active service again and tells them where to respond for the next alarm. If that location is far from that of the false alarm, then the distance and the time it takes to get to the new location are increased. This means that firefighters will arrive later to help in fighting the real fire and the fire will have more time to burn. The fire will be bigger and more dangerous just because someone called the firefighters to a false alarm. In addition, each time the firefighters ride to the location of a false alarm, there is additional risk of unnecessary accidents and injuries to them and to citizens.

11. The MAIN point of the above passage is that false alarms

   A. seldom interrupt other activities in the firehouse
   B. occur more often during the winter

C. are rarely turned in by children
D. add more risk of danger to life and property

12. When firefighters are called to a false alarm, they must NOT respond to other alarms until they

    A. turn in a written report to the fire department
    B. take a vote and all agree to go
    C. are put back into active service by the fire department
    D. decide on the quickest route

13. Before firefighters get to the location of a reported fire, they

    A. finish eating their lunch at the firehouse
    B. do not know if the alarm is real or false
    C. search the neighborhood for the person who made the report
    D. do not know if the alarm is from an alarm box or telephone

14. The above passage states that false alarms

    A. shorten travel time to real fires
    B. give firefighters needed driving practice
    C. save money on fuel for the fire department
    D. account for about 48% of reported fires

Questions 15-18.

DIRECTIONS: Questions 15 through 18 are to be answered SOLELY on the basis of the following passage.

Fires in vacant buildings are a major problem for firefighters. People enter vacant buildings to remove building material or they damage stairs, floors, doors, and other parts of the building. The buildings are turned into dangerous structures with stairs missing, holes in the floors, weakened walls and loose bricks. Children and arsonists find large amounts of wood, paper, and other combustible materials in the buildings and start fires which damage and weaken the buildings even more. Firefighters have been injured putting out fires in these buildings due to these dangerous conditions. Most injuries caused while putting out fires in vacant buildings could be eliminated if all of these buildings were repaired. All such injuries could be eliminated if the buildings were demolished. Until then, firefighters should take extra care while putting out fires in vacant buildings.

15. The problem of fires in vacant buildings could be solved by

    A. repairing buildings
    B. closing up the cellar door and windows with bricks and cement
    C. arresting suspicious persons before they start the fires
    D. demolishing the buildings

16. Firefighters are injured putting out fires in vacant buildings because

    A. there are no tenants to help fight the fires
    B. conditions are dangerous in these buildings

C. they are not as careful when nobody lives in the buildings
D. the water in the buildings has been turned off

17. Vacant buildings often have

   A. occupied buildings on either side of them
   B. safe empty spaces where neighborhood children can play
   C. combustible materials inside them
   D. strong walls and floors that cannot burn

18. While firefighters are putting out fires in vacant buildings, they should

   A. be extra careful of missing stairs
   B. find the children who start the fires
   C. learn the reasons why the fires are set
   D. help to repair the buildings

Questions 19-20.

DIRECTIONS: Questions 19 and 20 are to be answered SOLELY on the basis of the following passage.

Firefighters inspect many different kinds of places to find fire hazards and have them reviewed. During these inspections, the firefighters try to learn as much as possible about the place. This knowledge is useful should the firefighters have to fight a fire at some later date at that location. When inspecting subways, firefighters are much concerned with the effects a fire might have on the passengers because, unless they have been trapped in a subway car during a fire, most subway riders do not think about the dangers involved in a fire in the subway. During a fire, the air in cars crowded with passengers may become intensely hot. The cars may fill with dense smoke. Lights may dim or go out altogether, leaving the passengers in darkness. Ventilation from fans and air conditioning may stop. The train may be stuck and unable to be moved through the tunnel to a station. Fear may send the trapped passengers into a panic. Firefighters must protect the passengers from the fire, heat, and smoke, calm them down, get them out quickly to a safe area, and put out the fire. To do this, firefighters may have to climb from street level down into the subway tunnel to reach a train stopped inside the tunnel. Before actually going on the tracks, they must be sure that the 600 volts of live electricity carried by the third rail is shut off. They may have to stretch fire hose a long distance down subway stairs, on platforms, and along the subway tracks to get the water to the fire and put it out. Subway fires are difficult to fight because of these special problems, but preparing for them in advance can help save the lives of both firefighters and passengers.

19. During a subway fire, a train is stuck in a tunnel. Firefighters have been ordered into the tunnel.
Before firefighters actually step down on the tracks, they must be sure that

   A. all the passengers have been removed from the burning subway cars to a safe place
   B. they have stretched their fire hose a long distance to put water on the fire
   C. live electricity carried by the third rail is shut off
   D. the train is moved from the tunnel to the nearest station

20. According to the above passage, fire in the subway may leave passengers in subway cars in darkness.
    This occurs MAINLY because

    A. the lights may go out
    B. air in the cars may become very hot
    C. ventilation may stop
    D. people may panic

Questions 21-25.

DIRECTIONS: Questions 21 through 25 concern various forms, reports, or other documents that must be filed according to topic. Listed below are four topics numbered 1 through 4, under which forms, reports, and documents may be filed. In each question, choose the topic under which the form, report, or document concerned should be filed.
1. Equipment and supplies
2. Fire prevention
3. Personnel
4. Training

21. Under which topic would it be MOST appropriate to file a letter on a heroic act performed by a member of the fire company?

    A. 1   B. 2   C. 3   D. 4

22. Under which topic should a firefighter look for information about the fire company's new portable ladder?

    A. 1   B. 2   C. 3   D. 4

23. Under which topic should a firefighter locate a copy of the fire company's fire prevention building inspection schedule for the current year?

    A. 1   B. 2   C. 3   D. 4

24. Under which topic should a firefighter file a copy of a report on company property which has been damaged?

    A. 1   B. 2   C. 3   D. 4

25. Under which topic should a firefighter be able to locate a roster of firefighters assigned to the company?

    A. 1   B. 2   C. 3   D. 4

KEY (CORRECT ANSWERS)

1. B
2. D
3. B
4. C
5. A

6. B
7. D
8. D
9. A
10. B

11. D
12. C
13. B
14. D
15. D

16. B
17. C
18. A
19. C
20. A

21. C
22. A
23. B
24. A
25. C

TEST 2

DIRECTIONS: Each question or incomplete statement is followed by several suggested answers or completions. Select the one that BEST answers the question or completes the statement. *PRINT THE LETTER OF THE CORRECT ANSWER IN THE SPACE AT THE RIGHT.*

1. Firefighters must check gauges on fire engines so that defects are discovered and corrected. Some fire engines are equipped with gauges called. *Chargicators,* which indicate whether or not the electrical system is operating properly. When the fire engine's motor is running, the chargicator of a properly operating electrical system will show a reading of 13.5 to 14.2 volts on the scale. Which one of the following gauges shows a PROPERLY operating electrical system?

1.____

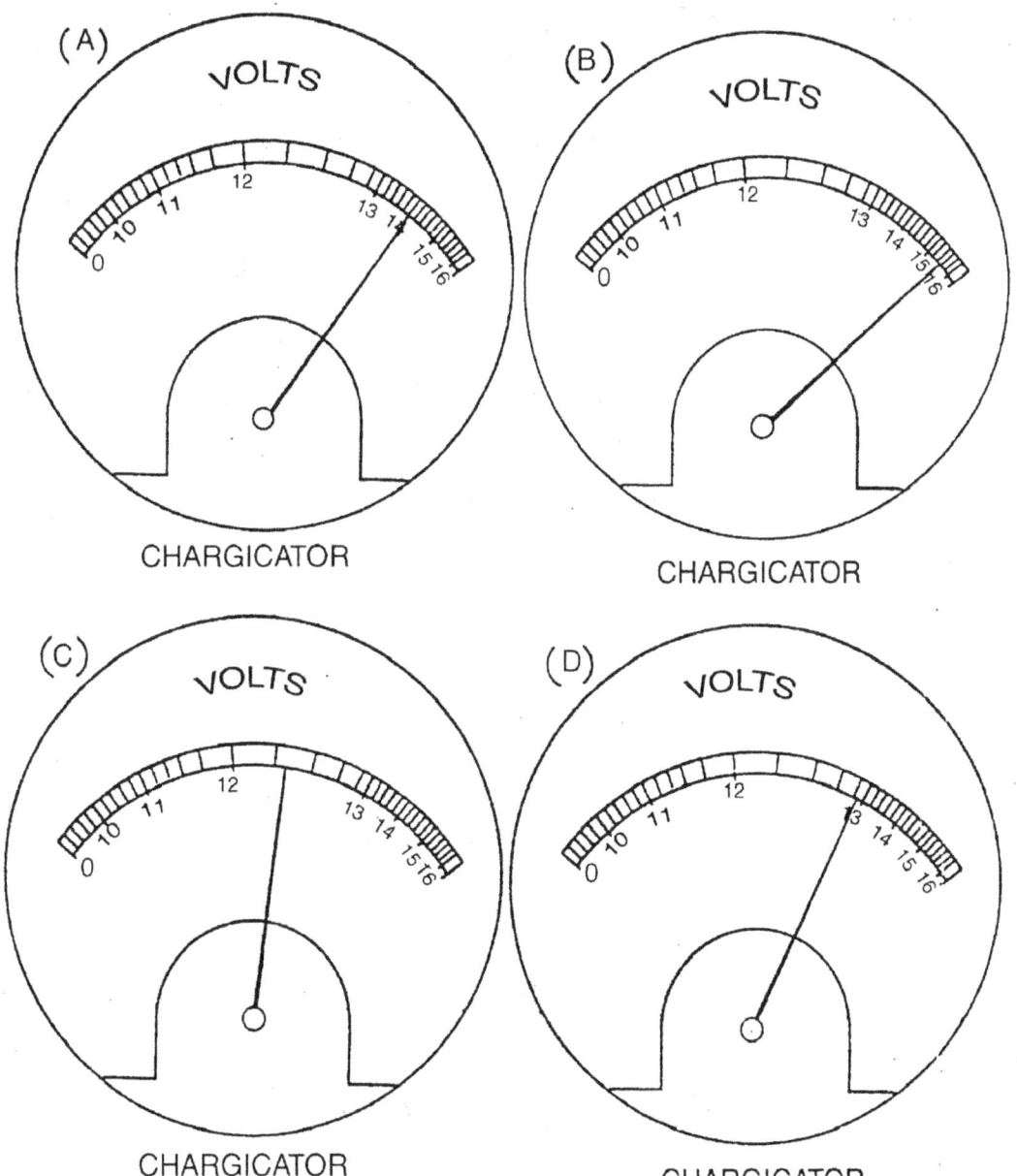

Questions 2-5.

DIRECTIONS: Questions 2 through 5 are to be answered SOLELY on the basis of the following facts and diagrams.

The gauges shown below in Diagrams I and II represent gauges on a fire engine's pump control panel at the scene of a fire. Diagram I gives the readings at 10 A.M., and Diagram II gives the readings at 10:15 A.M. Each diagram has one gauge labeled *Incoming* and one gauge marked *Outgoing*. The *Incoming* gauges show the pressure in pounds per square inch (psi) of the water coming into the pumps on the fire engine from a hydrant. The *Outgoing* gauges show the pressure in pounds per square inch (psi) of the water leaving the pumps on the fire engine. The pumps on the fire engine raise the pressure of the water coming from the hydrant to the higher pressures needed in the fire hoses.

DIAGRAM I

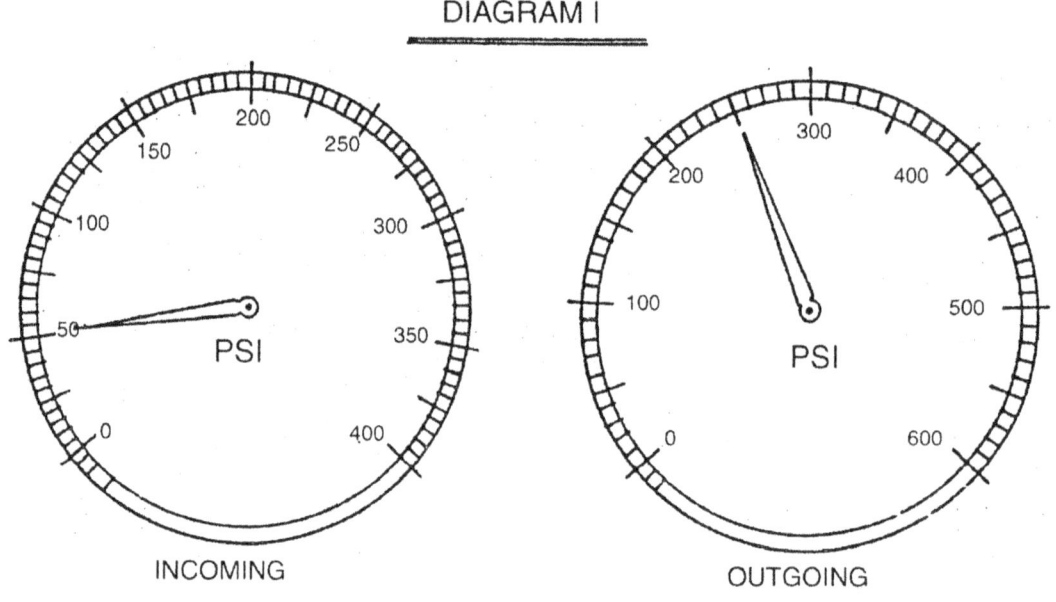

DIAGRAM II

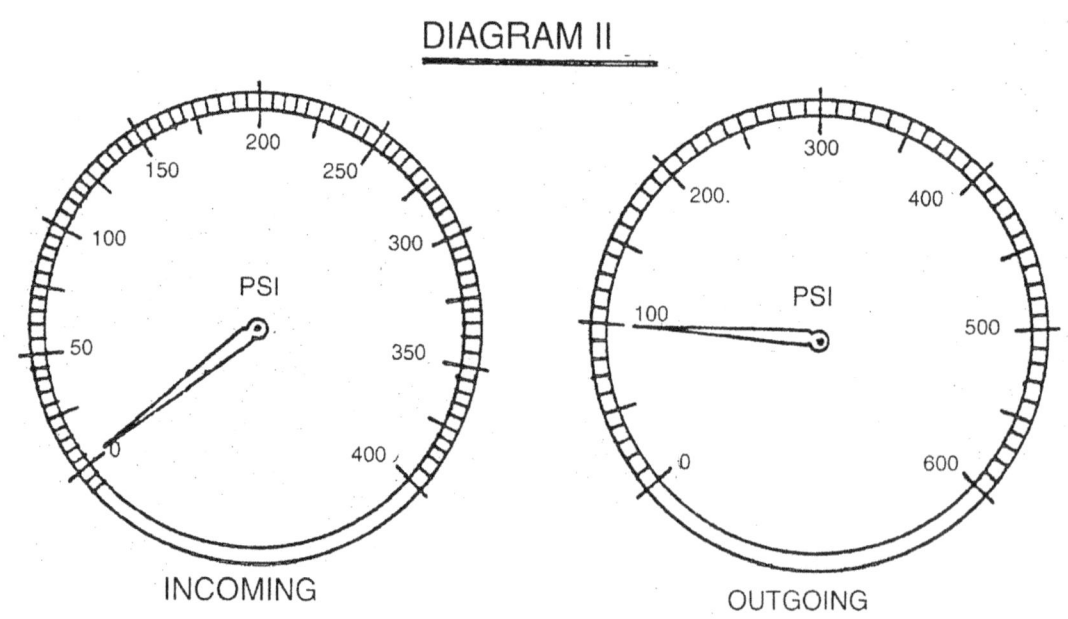

2. The firefighter looks at the gauges as shown in Diagram I and observes that the pressure, in pounds per square inch (psi), of the water coming into the pumps is MOST NEARLY

   A. 50   B. 250   C. 300   D. 500

3. The firefighter looks at the gauges shown in Diagram I and observes that the pressure, in pounds per square inch (psi), of the water going out of the pumps is MOST NEARLY

   A. 25   B. 50   C. 250   D. 500

4. Diagram II shows the incoming and outgoing water pressure fifteen minutes later. By looking at the gauges in Diagram II, the firefighter observes that the water _____ the pumps is _____ psi.

   A. going out of; at, 200
   B. going out of; at 5
   C. coming into; above 10
   D. coming into; below 10

5. The firefighter is able to determine that, between the time of Diagram I and the time of Diagram II, the pressure of the outgoing water from the pumps _____ by _____ psi.

   A. *increased;* 50
   B. *decreased;* 150
   C. *decreased;* 45
   D. *increased;* 145

Questions 6-11.

DIRECTIONS: Questions 6 through 11 are to be answered SOLELY on the basis of the following information.

In order to extinguish fires, firefighters must pull enough hose from the fire engine to reach the fire. Each length of hose is 50 feet long. The lengths of hose are attached together so that the water can go from the pump on the fire engine to a position where it will extinguish the fire.

6. If the total distance to reach the fire is 50 feet, what is the MINIMUM number of lengths of hose needed?

   A. 1   B. 2   C. 4   D. 4

7. If the total distance to reach the fire is 250 feet, what is the MINIMUM number of lengths of hose needed?

   A. 3   B. 4   C. 5   D. 6

8. If the total distance to reach the fire is 175 feet, what is the MINIMUM number of lengths of hose needed?

   A. 2   B. 3   C. 4   D. 5

9. If the total distance to reach the fire is 125 feet, what is the MINIMUM number of lengths of hose needed?

   A. 2   B. 3   C. 4   D. 5

10. If the total distance to reach the fire is 315 feet, what is the MINIMUM number of lengths of hose needed?   10.___

   A. 3   B. 5   C. 6   D. 7

11. If the total distance to reach the fire is 230 feet, what is the MINIMUM number of lengths of hose needed?   11.___

   A. 4   B. 5   C. 6   D. 7

Questions 12-13.

DIRECTIONS: Questions 12 and 13 are to be answered SOLELY on the basis of the following passage and diagrams.

Firefighters breathe through an air mask to protect their lungs from dangerous smoke when fighting fires. The air for the mask comes from a cylinder which the firefighter wears. A full cylinder contains 45 cubic feet of air when pressurized to 4500 pounds per square inch.

12. A gauge that firefighters read to tell how much air is left in the cylinder is pictured in the diagram at the right. The gauge indicates that the cylinder is   12.___
   A. full
   B. empty
   C. more than 3/4 full
   D. less than 1/2 full

13. A gauge which is part of the cylinder shows the pressure of the air in the cylinder in hundreds of pounds per square inch.   13.___
Which of the following diagrams shows a cylinder which is more than half full?

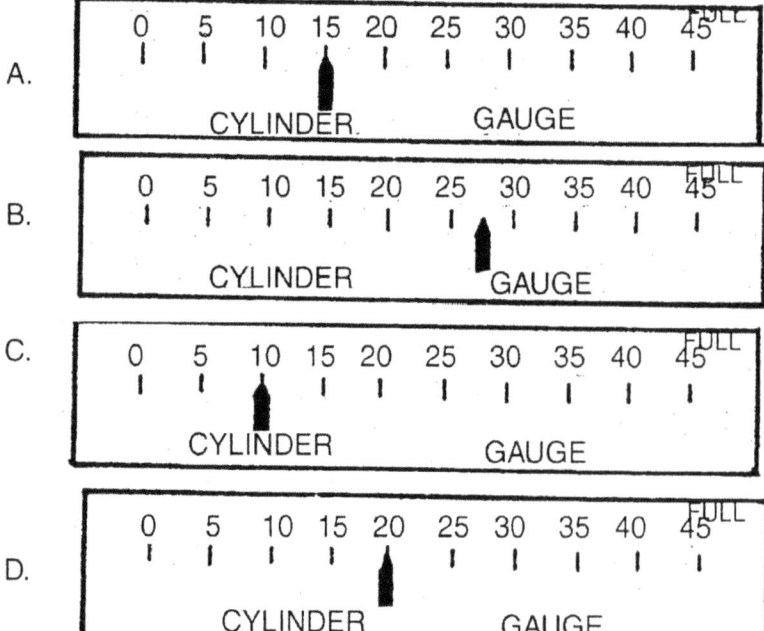

Questions 14-15.

DIRECTIONS: Questions 14 and 15 are to be answered SOLELY on the basis of the following passage.

The Fire Department uses a firehose nozzle with an automatically adjusting tip. The automatically adjusting nozzle tip keeps the water pressure at the tip constant even though the amount of water being pumped through the hose from the fire engine may vary. A partial loss of water in the hoseline does not result in the stream of water from the nozzle falling short of the target. A partial loss of water is caused by a kink in the hose somewhere between the fire engine pumping the water and the nozzle or by insufficient pressure being supplied by the fire engine pumping water into the hoseline.

The danger of this automatic nozzle is that as the nozzle tip adjusts to maintain constant water pressure, the number of gallons of water per minute flowing out of the nozzle is reduced. When the number of gallons of water per minute flowing from the nozzle is reduced, the nozzle is easier to handle and the stream of water coming from the nozzle appears to be adequate. However, since the number of gallons of flow is reduced, the cooling power of the hose stream will probably not be enough to fight the fire. If a firefighter can physically handle the hoseline alone, the nozzle is not discharging enough water, even though the stream coming out of the nozzle appears adequate. An adequate fire stream requires two firefighters to handle the hoseline.

14. An officer tells a firefighter to check why enough water is not coming out of a hoseline equipped with an automatic nozzle. The firefighter follows the hoseline from the nozzle back to the fire engine pumping the water into the hose but finds no kinks in the hose. The firefighter should inform the officer that the inadequate flow of water is PROBABLY due to

   A. a defective automatic nozzle
   B. the nozzle stream being aimed in the wrong direction
   C. insufficient pressure being supplied by the fire engine pumping water into the hoseline
   D. the fire engine not being connected to a hydrant

14.____

15. One firefighter alone is easily handling a hoseline equipped with an automatic nozzle. The hoseline's stream is reaching the fire.
According to the above passage, the firefighter should PROPERLY conclude that

   A. being able to handle the hoseline alone indicates extreme strength and excellent physical condition
   B. the stream of water coming from the nozzle is probably not an acceptable firefighting stream because not enough water is flowing
   C. the stream of water coming from the nozzle is adequate and is helping to save water
   D. the automatic nozzle has adjusted itself to provide the proper amount of water to fight the fire

15.____

Questions 16-17.

DIRECTIONS: Questions 16 and 17 are to be answered SOLELY on the basis of the following passage.

Firefighters at times are required to work in areas where the atmosphere contains contaminated smoke. To protect the firefighter from breathing the harmful smoke, a self-contained breathing mask is worn. The mask will supply the firefighter with a limited supply of pure breathing air. This will allow the firefighter to enter the smoke-filled area. The mask is lightweight and compact, which makes it less tiring and easier to move around with. The face mask is designed to give the firefighter the maximum visibility possible. The supply of breathing air is limited, and the rate of air used depends upon the exertion made by the firefighter. Although the mask will protect the firefighter from some types of contaminated smoke, it gives no protection from flame, heat, or heat exhaustion.

16. The rate at which the firefighter breathes the air from the mask will depend upon the

    A. amount of energy used by the firefighter
    B. amount of smoke the firefighter will breathe
    C. color of the flames that the firefighter will enter
    D. color of the heat that the firefighter will enter

17. According to the above passage, the mask will protect the firefighter from some types of

    A. flames   B. smoke
    C. heat   D. heat exhaustion

Questions 18-21.

DIRECTIONS: Questions 18 through 21 are to be answered SOLELY on the basis of the following passage.

In each firehouse, one firefighter is always on housewatch duty. Each 24-hour housewatch tour begins at 9 A.M. each day and is divided into eight 3-hour periods. The firefighter on housewatch is responsible for the correct receipt, acknowledgement, and report of every alarm signal from any source. Firefighters on housewatch are required to enter in the Company Journal the receipt of all alarms, as well as other matters required by Department regulations. All entries by the firefighter on housewatch should be written in blue or black ink. Any entries made by firefighters not on housewatch are made in red ink. Most entries, including receipt of alarms, are recorded in order, starting in the front of the Company Journal on Page 1.

Certain types of entries are recorded in special places in the Journal. When high level officers visit the company, those visits are recorded on Page 500. Company training drills and instruction periods are recorded on Page 497. The monthly meter readings of the utility companies which serve the firehouse are recorded on Page 493.

18. A firefighter is asked by the company officer to find out what alarms were received the previous day, August 25, between 1 A.M. and 2 A.M.
    Where in the Company Journal should the firefighter look to obtain this information?

    A. On Page 493
    B. Between Page 1 and Page 492, on the page for August 25
    C. On Page 500
    D. Between Page 497 and Page 500 on the page for August 25

19. A firefighter on housewatch is asked to find out how much electricity was used in the firehouse between the last two meter readings taken by Con Edison.
On which one of the following pages of the Company Journal should the firefighter look to find the last two electrical meter readings entered?

   A. 253 B. 493 C. 497 D. 500

20. A firefighter on housewatch duty is notified by a passing civilian of a rubbish fire around the block. The company responds, extinguishes the rubbish fire, and returns to the firehouse.
The firefighter on housewatch should

   A. make no entry in the Company Journal of the receipt of the alarm because it was received orally from the civilian
   B. record the alarm in red ink in the Company Journal
   C. record the alarm in blue ink in the Company Journal
   D. ask the civilian to record the alarm in red ink in the Company Journal

21. The company officer asks the firefighter on housewatch to find out the last date on which the company had a training drill on high-rise building fire operations.
On which one of the following pages of the Company Journal should the firefighter on housewatch look to find the date of the training drill?

   A. 36 B. 493 C. 497 D. 500

Questions 22-23.

DIRECTIONS: Questions 22 and 23 are to be answered SOLELY on the basis of the following passage.

Fire Department regulations require that upon receiving an alarm while in the firehouse, the officer of the fire company directs the firefighters to take positions in front of the firehouse. The firefighters warn pedestrians and vehicles that the fire engine is leaving the firehouse. The officer directs the driver of the fire engine to move the fire engine to the front of the firehouse and to stop to check for vehicles and pedestrian traffic. While the fire engine is stopped, the firefighters will get on, and the officer will signal the driver to go to the alarm location.

22. When do the firefighters who were sent to the front of the firehouse actually get on the fire engine?

   A. As the fire engine turns into the street leaving the firehouse
   B. As the fire engine slows down while leaving the fire-house
   C. Inside the firehouse, before the fire engine is moved
   D. After the fire engine has been moved to the front of the firehouse and stopped

23. When responding to an alarm, why are the firefighters sent out of the firehouse before the fire engine?
To

   A. make sure that the firehouse doors are fully opened
   B. go to the nearest corner to change the traffic signal

C. warn pedestrians and vehicles that the fire engine is coming out of the firehouse
D. give the firefighters time to put on their helmets and boots

24. When the engine oil drum in the firehouse is nearly empty, it must be replaced by a new drum full of oil. A firefighter gives the drum a kick. It sounds empty. The firefighter then checks the written log to see how many gallons of oil have been taken out of the drum so far. Checking the written log is

A. *unnecessary,* since the oil drum sounded empty when the firefighter kicked it
B. *necessary,* since the log should tell the firefighter exactly how much oil is left
C. *unnecessary,* since the firefighter should avoid paperwork whenever possible
D. *necessary,* since the firefighter should always try to keep busy with useful activity

25. The Fire Department provides each firehouse with such basic necessities as electric light bulbs. As the items are used up, new supplies are ordered before the old ones are all gone.
Of the following, the BEST reason for ordering more electric light bulbs before the old ones are all gone is to

A. decrease the amount of paperwork a firehouse company must complete
B. be sure that there are always enough light bulbs on hand to replace those that burn out
C. make sure that the firehouse has enough electric light bulbs to supply nearby firehouses
D. decrease the cost of providing electricity to the firehouse

KEY (CORRECT ANSWERS)

1. A
2. A
3. C
4. D
5. B

6. A
7. C
8. C
9. B
10. D

11. B
12. D
13. B
14. C
15. B

16. A
17. B
18. B
19. B
20. C

21. C
22. D
23. C
24. B
25. B

EXAMINATION SECTION
TEST 1

DIRECTIONS: Each question or incomplete statement is followed by several suggested answers or completions. Select the one that BEST answers the question or completes the statement. *PRINT THE LETTER OF THE CORRECT ANSWER IN THE SPACE AT THE RIGHT.*

1. When attempting to rescue a person trapped at a window, firefighters frequently use an aerial ladder with a rotating base. The rotating base allows the ladder to move up and down and from side to side. In a rescue situation, the ladder should be placed so that both sides of the ladder rest fully on the window sill after it has been raised into position. Which one of the following diagrams shows the PROPER placement of the rotating base in relation to the window where the person is trapped?   1.____

   A. A   B. B   C. C   D. D

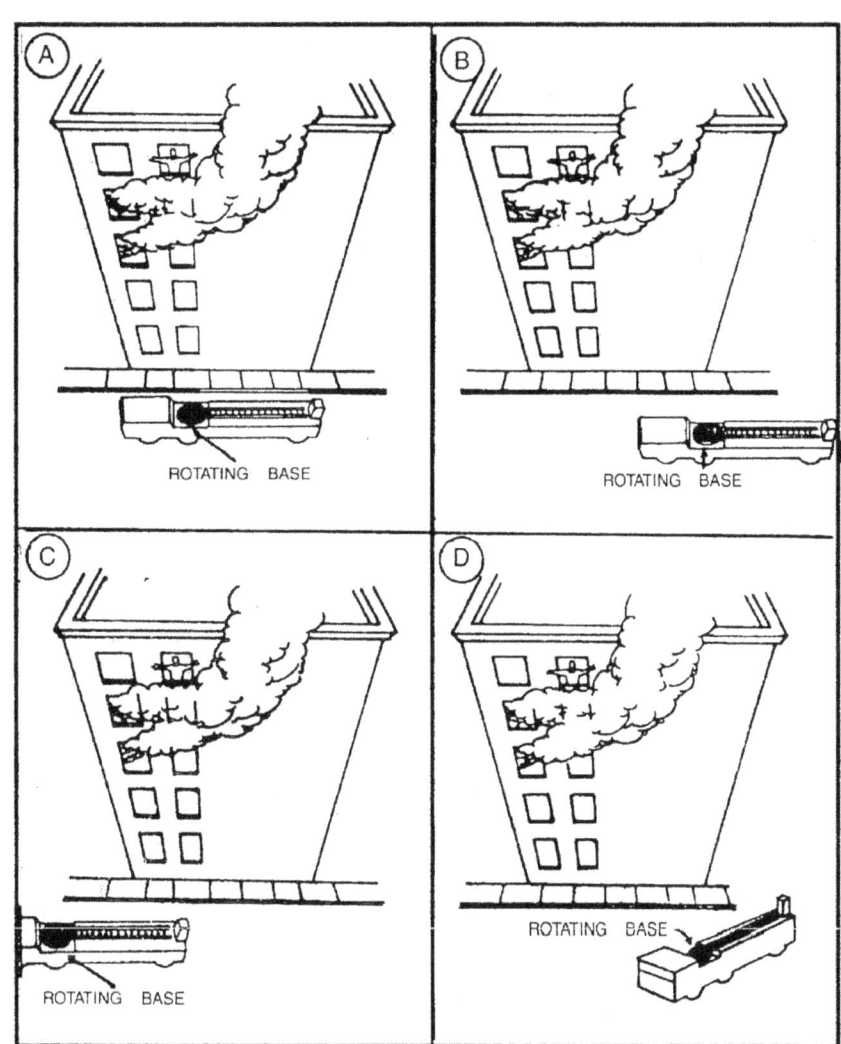

Questions 2-6.

DIRECTIONS: Questions 2 through 6 are to be answered on the basis of the following floor plan and information.

2 (#1)

Since many children may need to be rescued in the event of a school fire, city firefighters must become familiar with the floor layouts of public schools. Firefighters can develop this familiarity by conducting training drills at the schools.

A ladder company and an engine company recently conducted a drill at Pierce High School. The firefighters determined that the room layout is the same on all floors.

Several days after the drill, the ladder and the engine companies report to a fire at Pierce High School in classroom 304, which is on the third floor. The fire has spread into the hallway in front of Room 304, blocking the hallway.

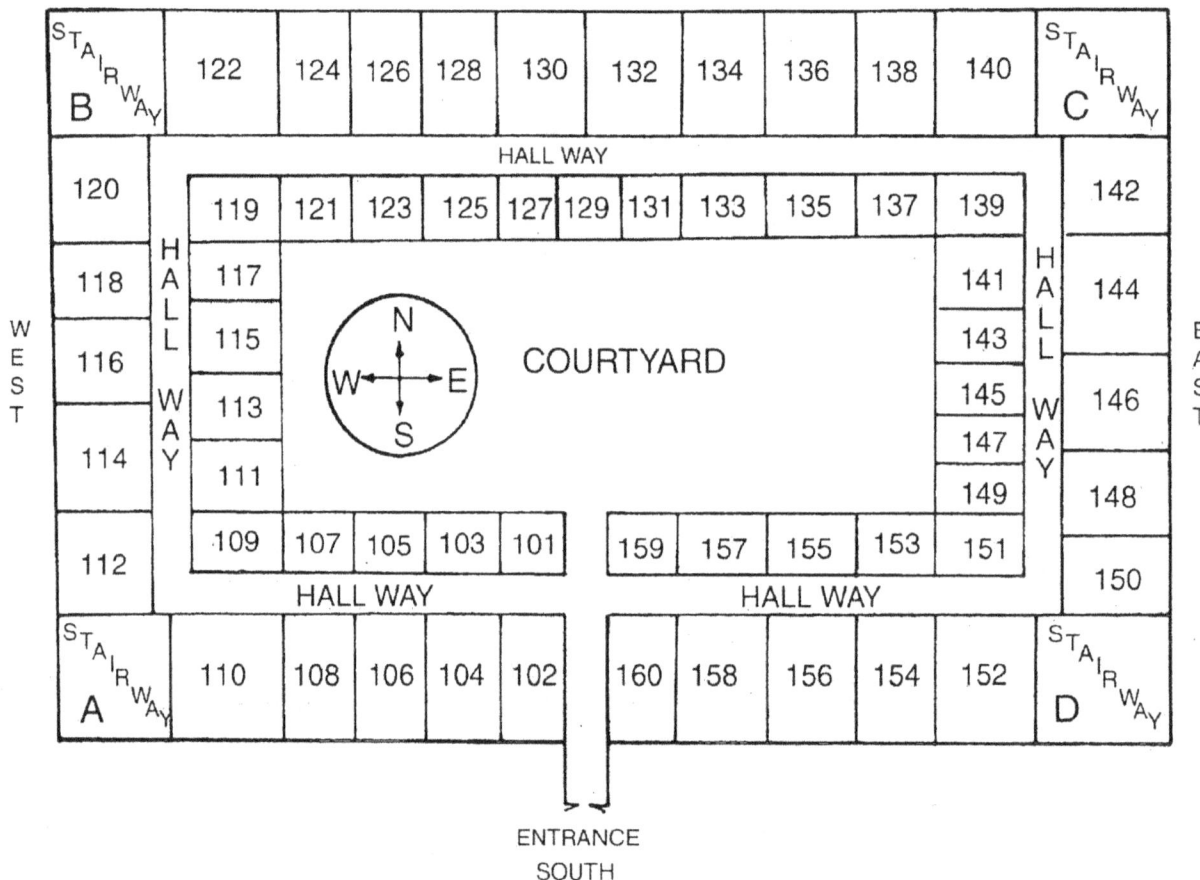

2. A firefighter is instructed to search for victims in the southwest area of the third floor. He wants to search as many rooms as possible and start his search as close to the fire as possible without passing through the fire. From the street, the firefighter should use his ladder to enter Room

  A. 302 B. 306 C. 312 D. 352

2.____

3. A firefighter goes to the third floor by way of the south-west building stairway. In Room 317, he finds a child who has been overcome by smoke. Upon returning to the hallway, he finds that the stairway he came up is now blocked by fire hoses.
   Which is the CLOSEST stairway that the firefighter can use to bring the child to the street level?

   A. A   B. B   C. C   D. D

4. Fire has spread from Room 304 to the room directly across the hall. As a result of heavy smoke, firefighters are ordered to break the windows of this room from the closest room on the floor above.
   Which room should the firefighters go to?

   A. 403   B. 305   C. 313   D. 413

5. The fire is in Rooms 303 and 305. Firefighters are told to go to rooms in the north corridor facing the courtyard that are directly opposite 303 and 305.
   Which rooms should the firefighters go to?

   A. 323 and 325   B. 326 and 328
   C. 333 and 335   D. 355 and 357

6. Another fire breaks out in Room 336, blocking the entire hallway. Firefighters have brought a hose up the north-east stairway to fight this fire. Another hose must be brought up another stairway so that firefighters can approach the fire from the same direction. What is the CLOSEST stairway that the firefighters could use?

   A. A   B. B   C. C   D. D

Questions 7-8.

DIRECTIONS: Questions 7 and 8 are to be answered on the basis of the following passage.

The firefighter who is assigned to the roof position at a fire in a Brownstone building should perform the following steps in the order given:

I. Go to the roof using one of the following ways:
   a. First choice - The aerial ladder
   b. Second choice - An attached building of the same height as the fire building
   c. Third choice - A rear fire escape
   d. Fourth choice - A thirty-five foot portable ladder

II. Upon arrival at the roof, look around to determine if any people are trapped who cannot be seen from the street.
   a. If a trapped person is observed, notify the officer and the driver that a life-saving rope rescue is required. While waiting for assistance to conduct this rescue, assure the victim that help is on the way and proceed to Step III.
   b. If no trapped persons are visible, proceed directly to Step III.

III. Remove the cover from the opening in the roof.
   a. If there is no smoke or very little smoke coming from the opening, report to the officer for further orders.
   b. If heavy smoke comes from the opening, proceed to Step IV.

IV. Remove the glass from the skylight.

7. Firefighters arriving at a fire in a Brownstone are using the aerial ladder to make an immediate rescue.
   The firefighter assigned to the roof position should go to the roof of the building on fire by

   A. a 35-foot portable ladder
   B. a rear fire escape
   C. an attached building of the same height
   D. the inside stairway of the fire building

   7.____

8. The firefighter assigned to the roof position at a fire in a Brownstone arrives at the roof and finds that no persons are trapped. He then removes the roof cover from the opening in the roof.
   Which one of the following steps should be performed next? He should _____ is coming from the roof opening.

   A. remove the glass from the skylight if heavy smoke
   B. remove the glass from the skylight if no smoke
   C. go to the top floor to assist in the search for trapped persons if heavy smoke
   D. report to the officer if heavy smoke

   8.____

Questions 9-10.

DIRECTIONS: Questions 9 and 10 are to be answered on the basis of the following passage.

Firefighters are often required to remove people who are trapped in elevators. At this type of emergency, firefighters perform the following steps in the order given:

1. Upon entering the building, determine the location of the elevator involved.

2. Reassure the trapped occupants that the Fire Department is on the scene and that firefighters are attempting to free them.

3. Determine if there are any injured people in the elevator.

4. Determine if all the doors from the hallways into the elevator shaft are closed.

5. If all the doors are closed, call for an elevator mechanic.

6. Wait until a trained elevator mechanic arrives before attempting to remove any trapped persons from the elevator, unless they can be removed through the door to the hallway. However, firefighters must remove the trapped persons by any safe method if any one of the following conditions exists:

   a. There is a fire in the building
   b. Someone in the elevator is injured
   c. The people trapped in the elevator are in a state of panic.

9. Firefighters arrive at an elevator emergency in an office building. When they arrive, a maintenance man directs them to an elevator which is stuck between the fourth and fifth floors. He informs the firefighters that there is a young man in the elevator who apparently is calm and unhurt.
Which one of the following steps should the firefighter perform NEXT?

   A. Determine if the young man is injured.
   B. Reassure the young man that the Fire Department is on the scene and that firefighters are attempting to free him.
   C. Check to make sure that all the doors to the elevator and hallways are closed.
   D. Call for an elevator mechanic and await his arrival.

10. Firefighters are called to an elevator emergency at a factory building. The freight elevator has stopped suddenly between floors. The sudden stop caused heavy boxes to fall on the elevator operator, breaking his arm. Upon arrival, the firefighters determine the location of the elevator. They tell the trapped operator that they are on the scene, are aware of his injury, and are attempting to free him. They determine that all the hallway doors leading into the elevator shaft are closed.
The firefighter's NEXT step should be to

   A. call for an ambulance and wait until it arrives
   B. remove the trapped person through the door to the hallway
   C. call for an elevator mechanic
   D. remove the trapped person by any safe method

11. The preferred order of actions for firefighters to take when removing a victim from an apartment on fire is as follows:
   1. First choice - Remove the victim to the street level through the public hallway.
   2. Second choice - Remove the victim to the street level by the fire escape.
   3. Third choice - Remove the victim to the street level using either a portable ladder or an aerial ladder.
   4. Fourth choice - Lower the victim to the street level with a life-saving rope.

   Firefighters answering an alarm are not able to use the entrance to a building on fire to reach a victim on the third floor because there is a fire in the public hallway. The victim is standing at the front window of an apartment on fire which has a fire escape. A firefighter places a portable ladder against the building, climbs the ladder, and enters the window where the victim is standing. The firefighter is carrying the life-saving rope and a 2-way radio. The radio allows her to communicate with the firefighter who operates the aerial ladder. The firefighter should then remove this victim from the fire apartment by using the

   A. fire escape B. aerial ladder
   C. portable ladder D. life-saving rope

12. Firefighters must regularly inspect office buildings to determine whether fire prevention laws have been obeyed. Some of these fire prevention laws are as follows: DOORS: Doors should be locked as follows:
   1. Doors on the ground floor may be locked on the street side to prevent entry into the stairway.
   2. Doors in office buildings that are less than 100 feet in height may be locked on the stairway side on each floor above the ground floor.
   3. Doors in office buildings that are 100 feet or more in height may be locked on the

stairway side except for every fourth floor.
The doors in an office building which is less than 100 feet in height may be locked on the stairway side

- A. on all floors including the ground floor
- B. on all floors above the ground floor
- C. except for every fourth floor
- D. on all floors above the fourth floor

13. SIGNS: Signs concerning stairways should be posted in the following manner:
    1. A sign shall be posted near the elevator on each floor, stating *IN CASE OF FIRE, USE STAIRS UNLESS OTHERWISE INSTRUCTED*. The sign shall contain a diagram showing the location of the stairs and the letter identification of the stairs.
    2. Each stairway shall be identified by an alphabetical letter on a sign posted on the hallway side of the stair door.
    3. Signs indicating the floor number shall be attached to the stairway side of each door.
    4. Signs indicating whether re-entry can be made into the building, and the floors where re-entry can be made, shall be posted on the stairway side of each door.

    Which one of the following CORRECTLY lists the information which should be posted on the stairway side of a door?
    A sign will indicate the

    - A. floor number, whether re-entry can be made into the building, and the floors where re-entry can be made
    - B. alphabetical letter of the stairway, whether re-entry can be made into the building, and the floors where re-entry can be made
    - C. alphabetical letter of the stairway and the floor number
    - D. alphabetical letter of the stairway, the floor number, whether re-entry can be made into the building, and the floors where re-entry can be made

14. Every firefighter must know the proper first aid procedures for treating injured people when there is a subway fire. In general, anyone suffering from smoke inhalation or heat exhaustion should be removed to fresh air and given oxygen immediately. Heart attack victims should be kept calm and should receive oxygen and medical attention immediately. Persons suffering from broken bones should not be moved until a splint is applied to the injury. However, in a situation where there is a smoky fire in the subway and the passengers needing immediate first aid are in danger from the fire, firefighters must first evacuate the passengers and perform first aid later, regardless of the injury.
    The PROPER first aid procedure for a man who has apparently suffered a heart attack on the station platform is to

    - A. have the man take the next train to the nearest hospital
    - B. remove the man to the street and administer oxygen
    - C. turn off the electrical power and evacuate the man through the tunnel
    - D. keep the man calm and administer oxygen

Questions 15-16.

DIRECTIONS: Questions 15 and 16 are to be answered SOLELY on the basis of the following passage.

A firefighter is responsible for a variety of duties other than fighting fires. One such duty is housewatch.

A firefighter's primary responsibility during housewatch is to properly receive alarm information. This enables firefighters to respond to alarms for fires and emergencies. The alarms are received at the firehouse by one of the following methods: computer tele-printer messages, Fire Department telephone or verbal alarm. The computer teleprinter and the telephone are used to alert the fire companies. These two types of alarms are transmitted by a dispatcher from a central communication office to the firehouse closest to the fire. The verbal alarm occurs when someone comes to the firehouse or stops the fire truck on the street to report a fire. Once an alarm has been received, the firefighter on housewatch duty alerts the rest of the firefighters to respond to the alarm.

Other housewatch responsibilities include keeping the appearance of the housewatch area neat and orderly, keeping the front of the firehouse clear of all vehicles and obstructions, and receiving telephone calls and visitors with complaints about fire hazards. The firefighter on housewatch duty also keeps an accurate and complete record of all administrative matters in a journal.

15. The methods a dispatcher uses to transmit alarms to the firehouse are the   15._____

    A. computer teleprinter, Fire Department telephone, and verbal alarm
    B. verbal alarm and computer teleprinter
    C. Fire Department telephone and verbal alarm
    D. computer teleprinter and Fire Department telephone

16. The PRIMARY responsibility of a firefighter on housewatch duty is to   16._____

    A. properly assign firefighters to specific duties
    B. properly receive alarm information
    C. keep the housewatch area neat and orderly
    D. write all important information in the company journal

Questions 17-18.

DIRECTIONS: Questions 17 and 18 are to be answered SOLELY on the basis of the following passage.

One duty of a firefighter on housewatch is to ensure that the computer teleprinter is working properly. A company officer should be notified immediately of any equipment problems. The firefighter on housewatch should check on the amount of paper in the teleprinter and should refill it when necessary. The firefighter should also check the selector panel on the computer. This selector panel has a series of buttons which are used by the firefighter to let the dispatcher know that an alarm has been received and that the fire company is responding. These buttons have lights. To check that the computer is functioning properly, the firefighter should press the button marked *test* and then release the button. If the computer lights go on, and then go off after the *test* button has been released, the computer is working properly. In addition, the light next to the *test* button should always be blinking.

17. In order to check that the selector panel of the computer is working properly, the firefighter on housewatch duty presses the button marked *test*, and then releases the button.
    The firefighter should conclude that the computer is working properly if the

    A. computer lights stay on
    B. computer lights keep blinking
    C. computer lights go on and then off
    D. *test* light stays on

18. A firefighter on housewatch duty notices that the tele-printer is almost out of paper.
    In this situation, the firefighter should

    A. test the computer panel by pushing the *test* button
    B. notify the officer to replace the paper
    C. place a new supply of paper in the teleprinter
    D. notify the dispatcher that the paper is being changed

Questions 19-20.

DIRECTIONS: Questions 19 and 20 are to be answered SOLELY on the basis of the following passage.

Following is a list of rules for fire extinguishers which are required in different types of public buildings in the city:

Rule 1: Hospitals, nursing homes, hotels, and motels must have one 2 1/2 gallon water extinguisher for every 2500 square feet, or part thereof, of floor area on each floor.

Rule 2: Stores with floor areas of 1500 square feet or less must have one 2 1/2 gallon water extinguisher. Stores with floor areas of over 1500 square feet must have one 2 1/2 gallon water extinguisher for every 2500 square feet, or part thereof, of floor area on each floor.

Rule 3: Kitchens must have one 2 1/2 gallon foam extinguisher or one 5 pound dry chemical extinguisher for every 1250 square feet, or part thereof, of floor area on each floor. For kitchen areas, this rule is in addition to Rules 1 and 2.

19. A firefighter is inspecting a one-story nursing home which has a total of 3000 square feet of floor area. This includes a kitchen, which is 1500 square feet in area, in the rear of the floor.
    Of the following, the firefighter should conclude that the nursing home should be equipped with

    A. 1 water extinguisher and 1 foam extinguisher
    B. 1 water extinguisher and 1 dry chemical extinguisher
    C. 2 water extinguishers and 2 foam extinguishers
    D. 2 foam extinguishers and 1 dry chemical extinguisher

20. A firefighter is inspecting a store which has two floors. The first floor has 2600 square feet. The second floor has 1450 square feet.
    The store should be equipped with AT LEAST

A. two 2 1/2 gallon water extinguishers, one for each floor
B. three 2 1/2 gallon water extinguishers, two for the first floor and one for the second floor
C. two 2 1/2 gallon foam extinguishers, one for each floor
D. two 2 1/2 gallon extinguishers, either foam or water, one for each floor

21. Firefighters from the first arriving ladder company work in teams while fighting fires in private homes. The inside team enters the building through the first floor entrance and then searches the first floor for victims. The outside team uses ladders to enter upper level windows for a quick search of the bedrooms on the second floor and above. The assignments for the members of the outside team are as follows:

    Roof person - This member places a ladder at the front porch and enters the second floor windows from the roof of the porch.

    Outside vent person and driver - These members work together and place a portable ladder at a window on the opposite side of the house from which the roof person is working. However, if the aerial ladder can be used, the outside vent person and driver climb the aerial ladder in the front of the house and the roof person places a portable ladder on the left side of the house.

    In order to search all four sides of a private home on the upper levels, firefighters from the second arriving ladder company place portable ladders at the sides of the house not covered by the first ladder company, and enter the home through the upper level windows.

    The second ladder company to arrive at a fire in a 2-story private home sees the aerial ladder being raised to the front porch roof.

    In this situation, the firefighters should place their portable ladders to the

    A. left and right sides of the house since there is a front porch
    B. rear and right sides of the house since the aerial ladder is being used
    C. rear and left sides of the house since there is a front porch
    D. left and right sides of the house since the aerial ladder is being used

21.____

22. The priority for the removal of a particular victim by aerial ladder depends on the following conditions:

    If two victims are at the same window and are not seriously endangered by spreading fire, the victim who is easier to remove is taken down the ladder first and helped safely to the street. In general, the term *easier to remove* refers to the victim who is more capable of being moved and more able to cooperate. After the easier removal is completed, time can be spent on the more difficult removal.

    If there are victims at two different windows, the aerial ladder is first placed to remove the victims who are the most seriously endangered by the fire. The ladder is then placed to remove the victims who are less seriously exposed to the fire.

    Assume that you are working at a fire and that there are a total of three victims at two windows. Victims #1 and #2 are at the same window, which is three floors above the fire and shows no evidence of heat or smoke. Victim #1 is a disabled, 23-year-old male, and Victim #2 is a 40-year-old woman. Victim #3, a 16-year-old male, is at a window of the apartment on fire. From your position in the street, you can see heavy smoke coming from this window and flames coming out of the window next to it, Which one of the following is the PROPER order for victim removal? Victim

    A. #3, #2, #1   B. #1, #2, #3
    C. #1, #3, #2   D. #3, #1, #2

22.____

Questions 23-24.

DIRECTIONS: Questions 23 and 24 are to be answered SOLELY on the basis of the following passage.

The four different types of building collapses are as follows:

1. <u>Building Wall Collapse</u> - An outside wall of the building collapses but the floors maintain their positions.
2. <u>Lean-to Collapse</u> - One end of a floor collapses onto the floor below it. This leaves a sheltered area on the floor below.
3. <u>Floor Collapse</u> - An entire floor falls to the floor below it but large pieces of machinery in the floor below provide spaces which can provide shelter.
4. <u>Pancake Collapse</u> - A floor collapses completely onto the floor below it, leaving no spaces. In some cases, the force of this collapse causes successive lower floors to collapse.

23. The MOST serious injuries are likely to occur at _____ collapses. 23._____

    A. pancake B. lean-to
    C. floor   D. building wall

24. Of the following, a floor collapse is MOST likely to occur in a 24._____

    A. factory building   B. private home
    C. apartment building D. hotel

25. Many subway tunnels contain a set of three rails used for train movement. The subway trains run on two rails. The third rail carries electricity and is the source of power for all trains. Electricity travels from the third rail through metal plates called contact shoes which are located near the wheels on every train car. Electricity then travels through the contact shoes into the train's motor. Firefighters must be very careful when operating near the third rail because contact with the third rail can result in electrocution. 25._____
From the above, it is apparent that the source of power for subway trains is the

    A. third rail   B. contact shoes
    C. motor   D. metal plates

KEY(CORRECT ANSWERS)

1. A	11. A
2. B	12. B
3. B	13. A
4. A	14. D
5. A	15. D
6. D	16. B
7. C	17. C
8. A	18. C
9. B	19. C
10. C	20. B

21. B
22. A
23. A
24. A
25. A

TEST 2

DIRECTIONS: Each question or incomplete statement is followed by several suggested answers or completions. Select the one that BEST answers the question or completes the statement. *PRINT THE LETTER OF THE CORRECT ANSWER IN THE SPACE AT THE RIGHT.*

Questions 1-5.

DIRECTIONS: Questions 1 through 5 are to be answered SOLELY on the basis of the following passage.

    Firefighters receive an alarm for an apartment fire on the fourth floor of a 14-story housing project at 1191 Park Place. One firefighter shouts the address as the other firefighters are getting on the fire truck. Knowledge of the address helps the firefighters decide which equipment to pull off the fire truck when they reach the fire scene.
    The firefighters know where the water outlets are located in the building on fire. There is an outlet in every hallway. Firefighters always attach the hose at the closest outlet on the floor below the fire.
    As they arrive at 1191 Park Place, three firefighters immediately take one length of hose each and go into the building. Since an officer has been told by the dispatcher that two children are trapped in the rear bedroom, the officer and two firefighters begin searching for victims and opening windows immediately upon entering the apartment on fire.
    As in all housing project fires, the roof person goes to the apartment above the apartment on fire. From this position, he attaches a tool to a rope in order to break open the windows of the apartment on fire. From this position, the roof person could also make a rope rescue of a victim in the apartment on fire.

1. A firefighter shouted the address of the fire when the alarm was received so that the firefighters would

   A. know which equipment to take from the truck at the fire scene
   B. be more alert when they arrived at the fire
   C. be prepared to make a rope rescue
   D. know that two children were reported to be trapped

2. The hose should be attached to an outlet on the

   A. floor above the fire   B. ground floor
   C. fire floor   D. floor below the fire

3. Because of the information given to the officer by the dispatcher, the officer and two firefighters

   A. entered the apartment above the fire for a rope rescue
   B. began immediately to search for victims and to open windows
   C. opened all the windows before the hose was moved in
   D. attached a hose and moved to the origin of the fire

4. The roof person broke the windows of the apartment on fire with a(n)

   A. axe while leaning out of the windows
   B. axe attached to the end of a rope

C. tool while standing on the roof
D. tool attached to a rope

5. The PROPER location for a rescue by the roof person at a fire in a housing project is the   5.____

    A. hallway
    B. apartment below the apartment on fire
    C. apartment above the apartment on fire
    D. fire escape

6. Firefighters may have to use tools to force open an entrance door. Before the firefighters   6.____
   use the tools, they should turn the doorknob to see if the door is unlocked.
   If the door is locked, one firefighter should use an axe and the other firefighter should
   use a halligan tool. This tool is used to pry open doors and windows. Firefighters must
   take the following steps in the order given to force open the door:
      I. Place the prying end of the halligan tool approximately six inches above or
         below the lock. If there are two locks, the halligan tool should be placed
         between them.
      II. Tilt the halligan tool slightly downward so that a single point on the prying
          end is at the door's edge.
      III. Strike the halligan tool with the axe until the first point is driven in between
           the door and the door frame.
      IV. Continue striking with the axe until the door and frame are spread apart and
          the lock is broken.
      V. Apply pressure toward the door and the door will spring open.
   Firefighters respond to a fire on the second floor of a 3-story apartment building. Two
   firefighters, one equipped with an axe and the other with a halligan tool, climb the stairs
   to the apartment on fire. They see that there are two locks on the apartment door. The
   firefighters should now

    A. place the prying end of the halligan tool about six inches above or below the locks
    B. turn the doorknob to determine whether the door is locked
    C. tilt the halligan tool towards the floor before striking
    D. place the prying end of the halligan tool between the locks

7. You are a firefighter who is inspecting a building for violations. You must perform the fol-   7.____
   lowing steps in the order given:
      I. Find the manager of the building and introduce yourself.
      II. Have the manager accompany you during the inspection.
      III. Start the inspection by checking the Fire Department permits which have
           been issued to the building. The permits are located in the office of the build-
           ing.
      IV. Inspect the building for violations of the Fire Prevention Laws. Begin at the
          roof and work down to the basement or cellar.
      V. As you inspect, write on a piece of paper any violations you find and explain
         them to the building manager.
   You are inspecting a supermarket. After entering the building, you identify yourself to
   the store manager and ask him to come along during the inspection. Which one of the
   following actions should you take NEXT?

    A. Start inspecting the supermarket, beginning at the basement.
    B. Start inspecting the supermarket, beginning at the roof.

C. Ask to see the Fire Department permits which have been issued to the supermarket.
D. Write down any violations which are seen while introducing yourself to the manager.

Questions 8-9.

DIRECTIONS: Questions 8 and 9 are to be answered SOLELY on the basis of the following passage.

Engine company firefighters are responsible for putting water on a fire and extinguishing it. To do this properly, they should perform their tasks in the following order:

1. Once an apartment door has been forced open, the engine company officer orders the driver to start the flow of water through the hose.
2. As the water starts to flow into the hose, it pushes trapped air ahead of it. To clear this air from the hose, the nozzle is pointed away from the fire area, opened, and then closed before water starts to flow from it. This is done to prevent a rush of fresh air from the hose which will intensify the fire.
3. When the fire is found, the nozzle is directed at the ceiling to allow water to rain down on the fire. As the fire becomes smaller, the nozzle is aimed directly at the burning object.

8. When engine company firefighters enter an apartment where there is a fire, the occupant takes the firefighters to a fire in the bedroom.
Once air has been cleared from the hose, the firefighter operating the nozzle should

   A. wait for the ladder company to open the door
   B. aim water directly onto the bed
   C. spray the water across the floor
   D. direct the water at the ceiling and allow it to rain down on the fire

9. After the locked door at an apartment fire has been forced open and water starts to flow into the hose, the firefighter operating the nozzle sees an intense fire just inside the apartment doorway. She should then point the nozzle

   A. away from the fire
   B. directly at the fire
   C. at any burning object
   D. at the apartment floor

10. When a leak occurs in an oil pipeline, the Fire Department dispatcher sends a message for specific companies to respond to the leak. There is a letter code on the message indicating the possible location of the leak. After a firefighter reads the letter code on the message, the following steps are performed in the order given to properly close the valves on the pipeline:

    I. The firefighter looks up the alarm assignment card which gives the location of the valve.
    II. The firefighter makes sure that a short wrench and a long wrench are placed on the fire truck.
    III. Upon arrival at the location of the valve, the fire-fighter removes the steel valve cover with the short wrench.
    IV. The long wrench is then used to completely close the valve.

A firefighter receives a message from the dispatcher about a leak in an oil pipeline. After noting the letter code on the message, the firefighter should

- A. give the alarm card immediately to the officer in charge
- B. make sure the proper wrenches for closing the valve have been placed on the fire apparatus
- C. look up the alarm assignment card to determine the location of the valve
- D. remove the steel valve cover

11. When administering first aid to a person who is severely bleeding, firefighters should perform the following steps in the order given:
    I. Direct pressure
        a. Press a dressing directly on the wound
    II. Elevation
        a. Lift the injured body part above the heart level, while continuing direct pressure. This will slow down the movement of blood to the wound.
        b. Never elevate a body part if it might be fractured.
        c. If the bleeding continues while the injured body part is elevated and is receiving direct pressure, pressure should be applied to an artery or other pressure point.

A firefighter arrives at an automobile accident and finds a woman who is bleeding severely from a cut just above the ankle. She also has a fracture of the upper arm. After placing a dressing on the ankle wound, the fire-fighter should NEXT

- A. apply pressure to a pressure point to stop the bleeding
- B. elevate the upper arm and apply direct pressure to it
- C. apply direct pressure to an artery in the arm
- D. apply direct pressure to the leg while elevating it

12. One firefighter of the first company to arrive at a fire in a private house is assigned to the roof position. During the beginning stages of a fire, the roof person is part of a team which enters and searches the building for victims.
The roof person's duties are performed in the following order:
    I. Climb a portable ladder to the front porch roof, break a window, and enter the building through this opening if there is no victim in immediate danger visible at another window. If there is such a victim, place the ladder at that window.
    II. If there is no front porch, use the portable extension ladder at a side of the house.
    III. Enter the house after breaking a window.

The roof person at a fire in a private house sees a boy at a top floor window on the right side of the house. There is a porch in the front of the house. The roof person should now place the portable ladder at the

- A. front of the porch
- B. top floor front window
- C. top floor window, right side of the house
- D. top floor window, left side of the house

13. The following is a description of the actions taken by the outside vent person (O.V.) at different types of fires:

    Fire 1: At a fire at 3:00 A.M. on the third floor of a 5-story apartment building, the O.V. climbed the fire escape to break the windows in the fire area.
    Fire 2: At a fire at 1:00 P.M. on the fourth floor of a 4-story apartment building, the O.V. went to the roof to assist the firefighter assigned to the roof position.
    Fire 3: At a fire at 2:00 P.M. on the third floor of a 3-story factory building, the O.V. went to the roof to assist the firefighter assigned to the roof position.
    Fire 4: At a fire at 6:00 A.M. on the first floor of a 2-story clothing store, the O.V. broke the first floor windows from the outside of the building.
    Fire 5: At a fire at 1:00 A.M. on the fifth floor of a 5-story apartment building, the O.V. went to the roof to assist the firefighter assigned to the roof position.

    A firefighter should conclude that the O.V. assists the firefighter assigned to the roof position when the fire

    A. is in an apartment building
    B. occurs at night
    C. is located on the top floor of the building
    D. is in a commercial building

14. Firefighters perform both vertical and horizontal ventilation. In vertical ventilation, an opening is made on the upper levels of the fire building so that the natural air currents can assist in the removal of smoke and heated gases. In horizontal ventilation, windows are opened on the same level as the fire to allow fresh air into the fire area.
    A ladder company recently responded to the following fires at different 6-story apartment buildings and performed the actions indicated:

    Fire 1: At a fire in a mattress in a second floor apartment, firefighters immediately opened the roof door. After water began flowing through the hose, firefighters opened the windows in the apartment. The fire was quickly extinguished.
    Fire 2: At a fire in the top floor bedroom, firefighters cut a hole in the roof as soon as possible and then used the water from the hose to shatter the windows. The fire was quickly extinguished.
    Fire 3: At an apartment fire on the second floor, firefighters broke the windows in the apartment as the hose was being brought from the street. The fire spread before water could be applied to the fire.

    Based upon the types of ventilation performed at the three fires, which one of the following statements is CORRECT?

    A. Vertical ventilation must be performed by opening the roof door.
    B. Horizontal ventilation should be delayed until firefighters are ready to apply water to the fire.
    C. Horizontal ventilation must be performed before vertical ventilation.
    D. Vertical ventilation must be delayed until water is applied to the fire.

Questions 15-16.

DIRECTIONS: Questions 15 and 16 are to be answered on the basis of the following passage.

A newly appointed firefighter is studying the proper use of foam, water, or dry chemicals to extinguish a fire. The firefighter looks over past fire reports to see whether any patterns exist.

Fire 1: Gasoline fire near a car was extinguished by foam.
Fire 2: Fire in a television set with a disconnected power cord was extinguished by water.
Fire 3: Fire in a fuse box of a private home was extinguished by dry chemicals.
Fire 4: Oil fire near an oil burner in a private home was extinguished by foam.
Fire 5: Fire near the electrical rail at a subway was extinguished by dry chemicals.
Fire 6: Fire involving an electric range was extinguished by dry chemicals.
Fire 7: Fire in the front seat of an automobile was extinguished by water.

15. The firefighter should conclude that dry chemicals are used to extinguish fires which involve

    A. automobiles
    B. private homes
    C. oil and gasoline
    D. live electrical equipment

16. The firefighter should conclude that foam is used to extinguish

    A. car fires
    B. oil and gasoline fires
    C. stove fires
    D. electrical fires

17. In situations where there is no fire, firefighters must make immediate rescue attempts when they come upon persons in danger.
    Which one of the following persons to be rescued is in the GREATEST danger?
    A

    A. sleeping baby inside a car that has a leaking gasoline tank
    B. woman inside an elevator stuck on the 33rd floor
    C. teenage boy drifting on a lake in a boat
    D. woman confined to a wheelchair is locked in her apartment

18. Firefighters are inspecting a furniture factory. During the inspection, they find employees smoking cigarettes in various areas.
    In which area does smoking pose the GREATEST danger of causing a fire?

    A. Employee lounge
    B. Woodworking shop
    C. A private office
    D. A rest room

19. Firefighters should observe the sidewalk and street area in front of the firehouse and inform the officer of any conditions that may cause a significant delay when fire trucks must go out in response to an alarm.
    Which one of the following conditions should the firefighters report to the officer?

    A. A car is stopped in front of the firehouse for a red light.
    B. People are standing and talking in front of the firehouse.
    C. A truck is parked in front of the firehouse.
    D. There is a small crack in the sidewalk in front of the firehouse.

20. Which of the following conditions observed by a firefighter inspecting an automobile repair garage is the MOST dangerous fire hazard?

    A. A mechanic is repairing a hole in a half-filled gas tank while smoking a cigarette.
    B. A heater is being used to heat the garage.
    C. A mechanic is changing a tire on a van while smoking a pipe.
    D. There is no fire extinguishing equipment in the garage.

21. During a fire prevention inspection, a firefighter may find a condition which could be the immediate cause of death in the event of a fire.
Which one of the following conditions in a restaurant is the MOST dangerous?

    A. Blocked exit doors
    B. A crack in the front door
    C. A window that does not open
    D. A broken air conditioning system

22. It is very important to get fresh air into a closed area that is filled with gas or smoke.
In which one of the following situations should such an action be taken FIRST? A(n)

    A. smell of gas coming through an open apartment window
    B. unoccupied car with the motor running
    C. strong odor coming from a closed refrigerator
    D. gas leak in the closed basement of an occupied building

23. A firefighter who is assigned to the roof position at a fire must notify the officer of dangerous conditions which can be seen from the roof.
Which one of the following conditions is the MOST dangerous?

    A. The roof is sagging and may collapse because of the fire on the top floor.
    B. Rubbish is visible on the roof of the building next door.
    C. The stairway to the roof of the building has poor lighting.
    D. An automobile accident in the street is causing a traffic jam.

24. Firefighters must often deal with people who need medical assistance. In life-threatening situations, firefighters must perform first aid until an ambulance arrives. In less serious situations, firefighters should make the person comfortable and wait for the ambulance personnel to give first aid.
A firefighter should give first aid until an ambulance arrives when a person

    A. appears to have a knee injury
    B. is bleeding heavily from a stomach wound
    C. has bruises on his head
    D. has a broken ankle

25. At a fire on the west side of the third floor of a 10-story office building, a firefighter is responsible for rescuing trapped persons by means of the aerial ladder. The trapped person who is in the most dangerous location should be removed first.
Of the following, the firefighter should FIRST remove the trapped person who is

    A. on the rear fire escape on the east side of the second floor
    B. on the roof
    C. at a window on the west side of the fourth floor
    D. at a window on the tenth floor

KEY (CORRECT ANSWERS)

1. A
2. D
3. B
4. D
5. C

6. B
7. C
8. D
9. A
10. C

11. D
12. C
13. C
14. B
15. D

16. B
17. A
18. B
19. C
20. A

21. A
22. D
23. A
24. B
25. C

EXAMINATION SECTION
TEST 1

DIRECTIONS: Each question or incomplete statement is followed by several suggested answers or completions. Select the one that BEST answers the question or completes the statement. *PRINT THE LETTER OF THE CORRECT ANSWER IN THE SPACE AT THE RIGHT.*

Questions 1-10.

DIRECTIONS: Questions 1 through 10 are to be answered on the basis of the floor plan below. Study it for five minutes. Do not look at it again when answering the questions.

Firefighters must be able to find their way in and out of buildings that are filled with smoke. They must learn the floor plan quickly for their own safety and to help fight the fire and remove victims. Look at this floor plan of an apartment. There is an apartment on each side of this one. It is on the fifth floor of the building.

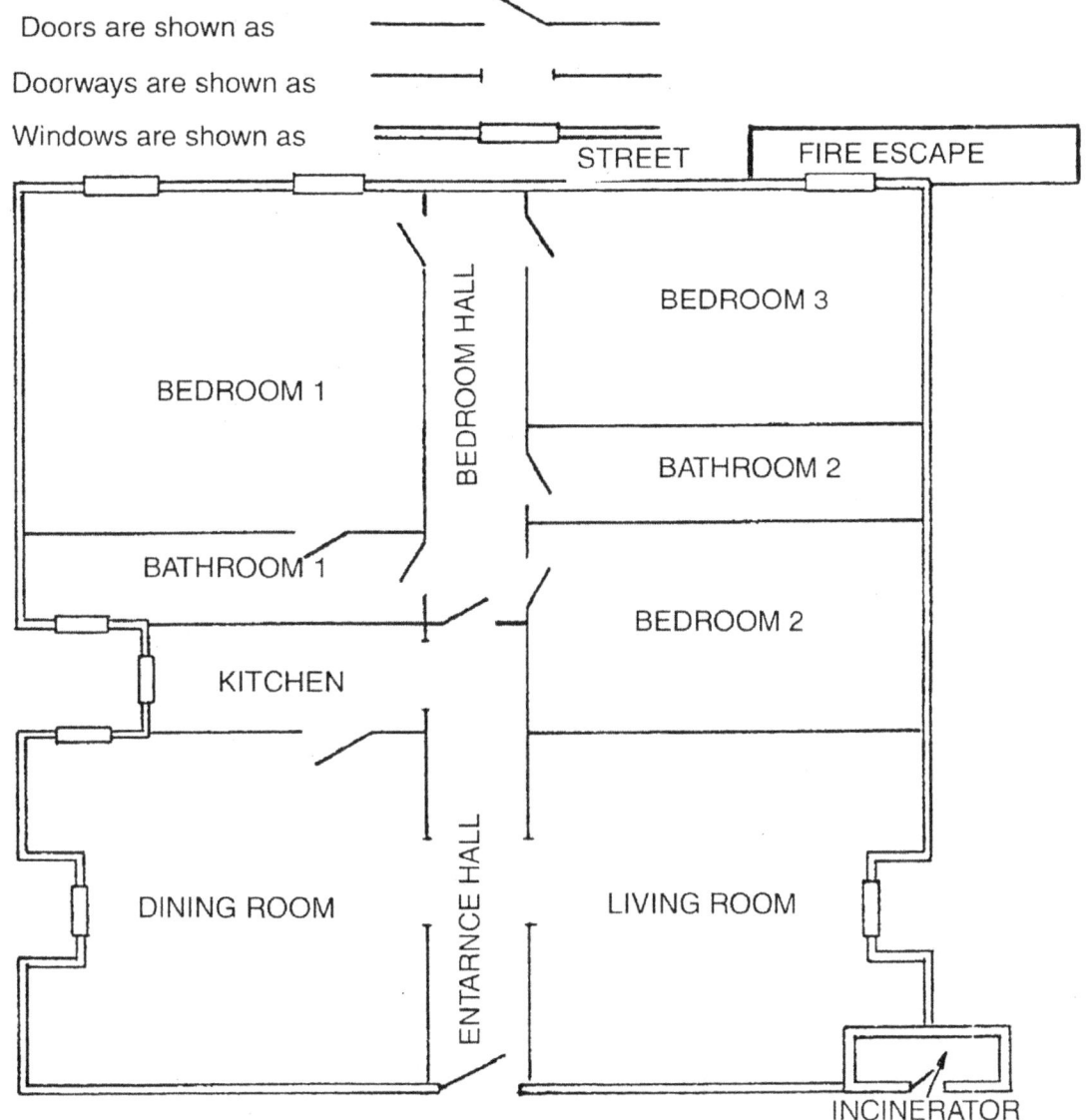

1. A person escaping a fire in the apartment can get on the fire escape by going through the window of

    A. Bedroom 1
    B. Bedroom 2
    C. Bedroom 3
    D. Living Room

2. If there is a fire in bedroom 3 and a firefighter is rescuing a child in bedroom 2, the SAFEST way of escape would be through the

    A. window of bedroom 2
    B. entrance hall and apartment door
    C. bedroom hall and bedroom 1
    D. bedroom hall and window of bathroom 2

3. Firefighters coming in the apartment's entrance door would have to go the LONGEST distance to get to the

    A. fire escape
    B. dining room
    C. door of bathroom 2
    D. kitchen window

4. Which one of the following rooms in the apartment CANNOT be closed off by a door?

    A. Living room
    B. Bedroom 1
    C. Bathroom 1
    D. Bedroom 2

5. A firefighter is in a room from which there is only one way of escape.
   Which one of the following rooms is the firefighter in?

    A. Living room
    B. Dining room
    C. Kitchen
    D. Bedroom 2

6. There is a fire in the apartment and the ladder of the fire truck in the street cannot be placed against the fire escape.
   The ladder should be raised from the street to reach a window in bedroom

    A. 1
    B. 2
    C. 3
    D. hall

7. A door from the kitchen leads directly into

    A. the dining room
    B. the living room
    C. bathroom 1
    D. the entrance hall

8. If a fire breaks through the walls of the incinerator, the people in the apartment NEAREST to the fire are those in

    A. bedroom 2
    B. bathroom 1
    C. the kitchen
    D. living room

9. Which one of the following choices lists two rooms which have NO windows?

    A. Bedroom 1 and bathroom 1
    B. Bedroom 2 and bathroom 2
    C. Kitchen and bathroom 2
    D. Living room and dining room

10. The door that can be closed to separate the bedrooms from the rest of the apartment is   10.____
    the door between the

    A. entrance hall and the bedroom hall
    B. living room and the entrance hall
    C. kitchen and the living room
    D. dining room and the living room

Questions 11-25.

DIRECTIONS: Questions 11 through 25 are to be answered SOLELY on the basis of the following facts and Building Inspection Form. Each box on the form is numbered. Read the facts and review the form before answering the questions.

Firefighters are required to inspect all buildings within their assigned area of the city. They check conditions within the building for violations of fire safety laws. While inspecting a building, they must fill out a Building Inspection Form as a record of the conditions they observed.

On June 12, 2007, Firefighter Edward Gold, assigned to Engine Company 82, is ordered by Captain John Bailey to inspect the building at 1400 Compton Place as part of the engine company's monthly building inspection duty. The building is a one-story brick warehouse where books of the S & G Publishing Company are stored before shipment to stores.

Firefighter Gold enters the warehouse through the main entrance door in the front of the building. Though an exit sign is present above the door, the sign is unlit because of a burned-out bulb. There is a small office to one side of the main entrance area where Firefighter Gold goes to meet the warehouse manager, Mr. Stevens. The firefighter explains the purpose of the inspection.

Firefighter Gold tells the manager that he will check the automatic sprinkler system first because if a fire got started in a warehouse full of stored books, the fire could spread rapidly. He asks Mr. Stevens for the Certificate of Fitness issued to the company employee certified to maintain the sprinkler system in working order. The certificate is dated June 1, 2004, and Gold observes that it has expired. The manager promises to have the certificate renewed as soon as possible.

The firefighter wants to locate the main control valve of the sprinkler system. He asks Mr. Stevens to go with him and show him its location. Gold and the manager leave through an office door which leads into the main working area of the warehouse. They locate the main sprinkler control valve on the wall in a corner of the work area behind high shelves stocked with books. The firefighter observes that the main control valve is sealed in the open position. Gold next climbs a ladder lying against the storage shelves and measures the distance between the top of the stack of books on the highest shelf and the sprinkler heads suspended on pipes below the ceiling. The distance is three feet.

Firefighter Gold next inspects the remaining exits from the building. A large fire door leads out to the loading dock in the rear of the warehouse. A small door on the side of the warehouse that is used by employees when they leave for the day is partially obstructed by cartons. Lighted exit signs can be clearly seen above both doors. During working hours, only the main entrance door and the fire door to the loading dock are unlocked. Mr. Stevens says

4 (#1)

he keeps the side door locked to keep employees from leaving early and only unlocks it at closing time.

Firefighter Gold and the manager then walk through the main work area. Gold observes that fireproof rubbish receptacles are placed at frequent intervals. However, they are not covered and the contents are overflowing, resulting in several piles of litter on the floor. *No Smoking* signs are on the walls of the work area, but are difficult to see behind the rows of high storage shelves.

The two fire extinguishers in the work area are found lying on the floor rather than hung on wall racks. The two other fire extinguishers in the warehouse, one in the office and one in the employee lounge, are both correctly hung on wall racks. All four fire extinguishers are fully charged. According to their tags, they were last inspected on March 11, 2007.

Firefighter Gold continues the inspection by checking on the electrical wiring, which appears to be generally in good condition. However, four switch boxes lack covers. The main junction box has a cover, but it cannot be closed because the cover is corroded.

The inspection is now complete, so Firefighter Gold thanks Mr. Stevens for his cooperation and leaves the building. Gold checks that all required information is entered on the Building Inspection Form, including information concerning building violations. Firefighter Gold signs and dates the Building Inspection Form and then submits it to Captain Bailey for his review. After reviewing Firefighter Gold's report, Captain Bailey signs the Building Inspection Form.

BUILDING INSPECTION FORM

DIVISION (1)	BATTALION (2)	COMPANY (3)	
BUILDING INFORMATION	Name of Business (4)	Address (5)	
	Type of Business (6)	Occupancy Code Number (7)	
CONDITION OF EXITS	Number of Exits (8)	Exits Obstructed (9)	Exits unlocked (10)
	Exit Signs (11)	Exit Sign Lights (12)	Fire Doors (13)
HOUSEKEEPING CONDITIONS	Rubbish Receptacles (14)	No Smoking Signs (15)	
	Clearance of Stock in Feet from Sprinkler Heads (16)		
	Electrical Wiring (17)	Switches (18)	Junction Box (19)
CONDITION OF FIRE EXTINGUISHERS	Charged (20)	Placement (21)	Date of Last Inspection (22)
CONDITION OF AUTOMATIC SPRINKLER SYSTEM	Color of Siamese (23)	Main Control Valve (24)	Shut-off sign (25)
	Certificate of Fitness (26)	Date of Last Inspection (27)	
SPECIAL CONDITIONS	Rubbish/Obstructions (28)	Certificate of Occupancy (29)	
		Heavy Load Signs (30)	
FIRE DEPARTMENT INFORMATION	Inspector Name ____ Signature ____ (31)	Rank (32)	Date (33)
	Officer Name ____ Signature ____ (34)	Rank (35)	Date (36)

11. Which one of the following should be entered in Box 3?

    A. Ladder Company 79
    B. Engine Company 12
    C. Ladder Company 140
    D. Engine Company 82

12. Which one of the following should be entered in Box 4? _____ Company.

    A. G & R Printing
    B. S & G Printing
    C. R & G Publishing
    D. S & G Publishing

13. Which one of the following should be entered in Box 8?

    A. 2   B. 3   C. 4   D. 5

14. Which one of the following should be entered in Box 9?

    A. Office door
    B. Side door
    C. Main door
    D. Fire door

15. Which one of the following should be entered in Box 10? _____ and _____ door.

    A. Fire; main
    B. Side; office
    C. Fire; side
    D. Main; cellar

16. The entry in Box 12 should show that replacement bulbs are needed for _____ light(s).

    A. one   B. two   C. three   D. all

17. The entry in Box 14 should show that covers are missing from _____ of the rubbish receptacles.

    A. two   B. three   C. four   D. all

18. Which one of the following should be entered in Box 16? _____ feet.

    A. One and one-half
    B. Two
    C. Two and one-half
    D. Three

19. Which one of the following should be entered in Box 19?

    A. Faulty circuits
    B. Exposed wiring
    C. Corroded cover
    D. Good condition

20. Which one of the following entries about the placement of fire extinguishers should appear in Box 21?

    A. One on the floor, three hung on wall racks
    B. Two on the floor, two hung on wall racks
    C. Three on the floor, one hung on wall rack
    D. Four hung on wall racks

21. Which one of the following should be entered in Box 22?

    A. June 1, 2004
    B. May 21, 2006
    C. March 11, 2007
    D. May 1, 2007

22. The entry in Box 24 should show that the position of the main control valve is   22._____

    A. open   B. half open
    C. one-third closed   D. closed

23. Which one of the following should be entered in Box 26?   23._____

    A. Expired   B. Missing from file
    C. Never issued   D. Current

24. Which one of the following should be entered in Box 28?   24._____

    A. Ceiling plaster cracked
    B. Rubbish piles litter work floor
    C. Second floor stairway blocked
    D. Open paint cans on loading dock

25. Which one of the following should be entered in Box 34?   25._____

    A. John Bailey   B. Edward Gold
    C. John Gold   D. Edward Bailey

KEY (CORRECT ANSWERS)

1. C	11. D
2. B	12. D
3. A	13. B
4. A	14. B
5. D	15. A
6. A	16. A
7. A	17. D
8. D	18. D
9. B	19. C
10. A	20. B

21. C
22. A
23. A
24. B
25. A

TEST 2

DIRECTIONS: Each question or incomplete statement is followed by several suggested answers or completions. Select the one that BEST answers the question or completes the statement. *PRINT THE LETTER OF THE CORRECT ANSWER IN THE SPACE AT THE RIGHT.*

Questions 1-8.

DIRECTIONS: Questions 1 through 8 are to be answered on the basis of the following items. The sizes of the items shown are NOT their actual sizes. Each item is identified by a number. For each question, select the answer which gives the identifying number of the item that BEST answers the question.

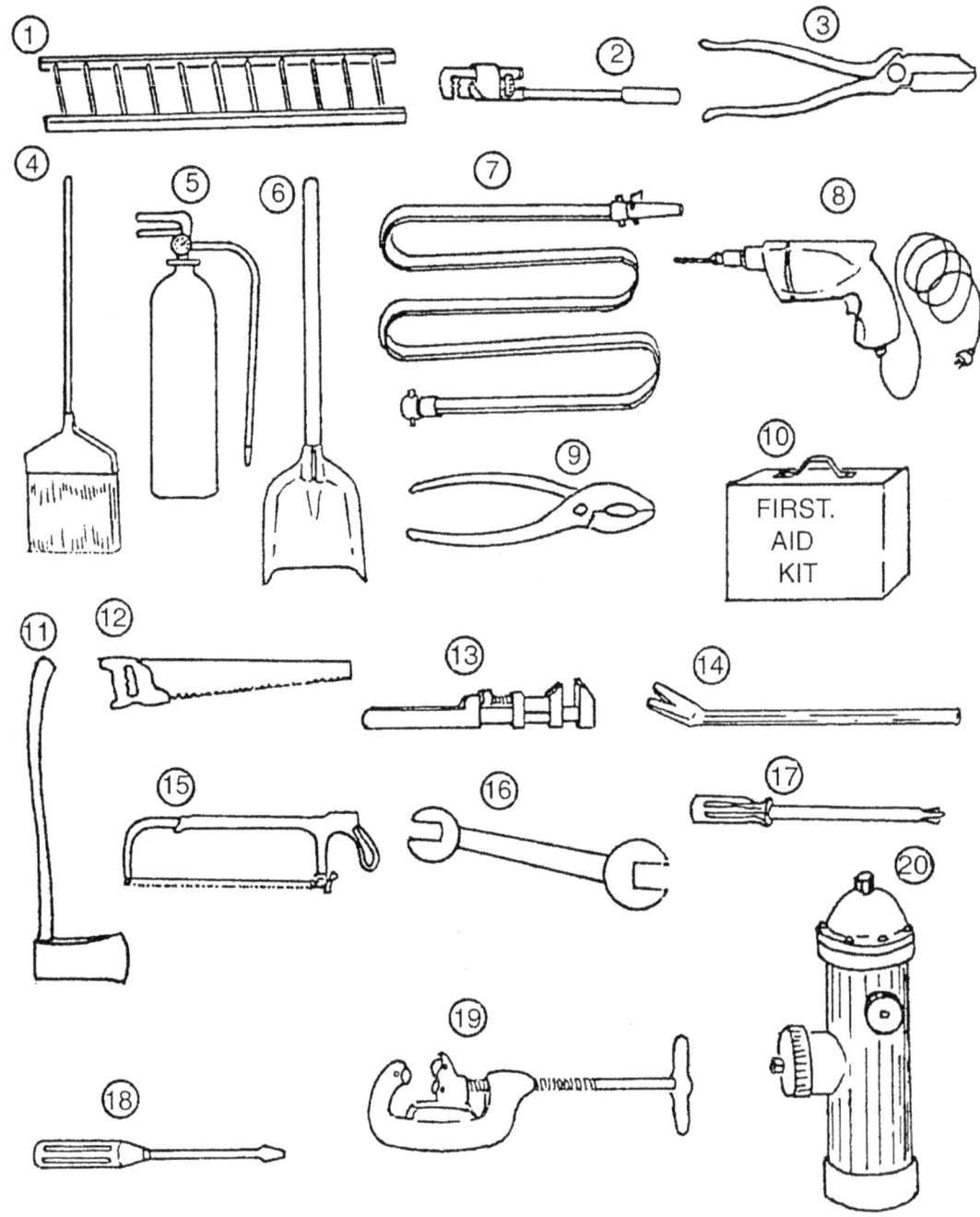

1. Which one of the following items should be connected to a hydrant and used to put out a fire?   1._____
   A. 5   B. 7   C. 8   D. 17

2. Which one of the following pairs of items should be used after a fire to clean a floor covered with small pieces of burned material?   2._____

3. Which one of the following pairs of items should be used for cutting a branch from a tree?   3._____
   A. 2 and 3   B. 8 and 9   C. 11 and 12   D. 14 and 15

4. Which one of the following items should be used to rescue a victim from a second floor window?   4._____
   A. 1   B. 10   C. 15   D. 20

5. Which one of the following pairs of items should be used to tighten a nut on a screw?   5._____
   A. 2 and 3   B. 8 and 19   C. 9 and 14   D. 16 and 18

6. Which one of the following items should be used to repair a leaky faucet?   6._____
   A. 4   B. 5   C. 12   D. 13

7. Which one of the following items should be used as a source of water at a fire?   7._____
   A. 2   B. 6   C. 9   D. 20

8. Which item should be used for cutting metal?   8._____
   A. 6   B. 13   C. 15   D. 18

9. An elderly man staggers into the firehouse and tells the firefighters on duty that he is having trouble breathing. Of the following, it would be BEST for the firefighters to   9._____
   A. send the elderly man away as his staggering shows that he has been drinking too much
   B. place the elderly man in a chair and quickly call for assistance
   C. tell the elderly man to go to the hospital and see a doctor
   D. help the elderly man leave the firehouse as this is not a problem that firefighters should handle

10. As firefighters travel to and from their firehouse, they usually look around the neighborhood in order to spot dangerous conditions. If they spot a dangerous condition, firefighters will take action to correct it. They do this because they want to prevent fires. While on his way to work overtime at a nearby firehouse, a firefighter passes a local gas station and spots a leaking gasoline pump.
    Which one of the following is the MOST appropriate course of action for the firefighter to take?   10._____
    A. Stop at the gas station and make sure that the leak is actually gasoline by lighting a match to it.
    B. Continue on to work because the gas station attendant will take care of the leak.
    C. Stop at the gas station and tell the gas station attendant to make sure the leak is repaired.
    D. Call the Mayor's Office to complain that the leaking gasoline is polluting the area.

11. A newly appointed firefighter is assigned to go with an experienced firefighter to inspect a paint store. The paint store owner refuses to allow the inspection, saying that he is closing the store early that day and going on vacation. The new firefighter demands rudely that the inspection be allowed, even though it would be permissible to delay it.
Of the following, it would be BEST for the experienced firefighter to

   A. repeat the demand that the inspection be allowed and quote the law to the store owner
   B. tell the new firefighter that it would be best to schedule the inspection after the store owner's vacation
   C. tell the store owner to step aside, and instruct the new firefighter to enter the store and begin the inspection
   D. tell the new firefighter to forget about the inspection because the store owner is uncooperative

11.____

12. The picture on the right shows a firefighter standing on a ladder. The firefighter should notice that a dangerous condition exists. Which of the following choices corresponds to the letter in the diagram showing the dangerous condition?
   A. The firefighter's coat is too long for safe climbing of the ladder.
   B. A helmet keeps the firefighter from seeing what is going on.
   C. The firefighter's feet are on the ladder rung.
   D. A ladder rung is missing.

12.____

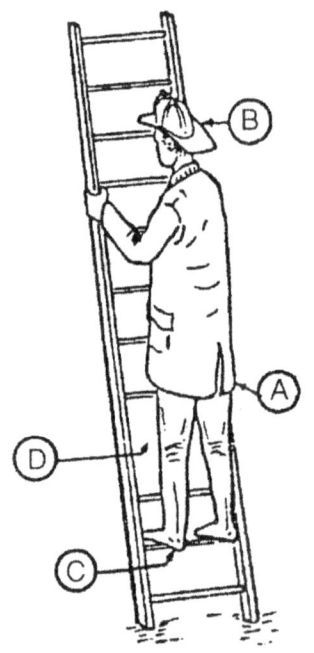

13. A firefighter is ordered to set up a hose on the street outside a building in which the second floor is on fire. The hose should be located about 30 feet from the building and should be aimed directly at the fire. Which one of the following diagrams shows how the firefighter should position the hose to aim it at the fire?

13.____

    A.   B.   C.   D.

   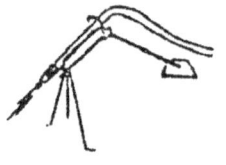

Questions 14-20.

DIRECTIONS: Questions 14 through 20 are to be answered SOLELY on the basis of the following information.

The portable power saw lets the firefighter cut through various materials so that a fire can be reached. It can be dangerous, however, if it is not properly used or if it has not been inspected and tested to insure that it is in serviceable condition. The parts of the saw should be clean and free of foreign material, especially the exhaust port and spark arrester, the carburetor enclosure, the cooling fins, the spark plugs, and the V-belt pulley if the saw has one.

The saw should be checked to make sure it has both air and fuel filters. It should never be run without an air filter. The V-belt pulley, if present, must be checked to make sure it is not too tight or too loose. If too loose, it could cause slipping. If too tight, the blade might turn when the engine idles, there might be damage to the clutch bearing, or the motor might stall when the blade is stopped. All nuts, bolts, and screws should be checked for tightness.

The saw may use carbide-tipped blades, aluminum oxide blades, or silicon carbide blades. Carbide-tipped blades should be returned for replacement when two or more tips are broken or missing or when the tips are worn down to the circumference of the blade. Aluminum oxide and silicon carbide blades should be replaced when they are cracked, badly nicked, or when worn down to an eight-inch diameter or less.

14. The PRINCIPAL reason for inspecting power saws is to make sure that 14.____

    A. they are clean
    B. they are in serviceable condition
    C. the pulley is not too tight or too loose
    D. the blades are replaced

15. What does the above passage mean when it says the saw should be kept free of foreign material? 15.____

    A. Only American-made parts should be used.
    B. The saw should not be used on material that might damage it.
    C. Both air and fuel filters should be used.
    D. Anything that does not belong on the saw or in it should be removed.

16. Some saws are made to work WITHOUT which one of the following items? 16.____

    A. An air filter   B. A fuel filter
    C. A V-belt pulley   D. Blades

17. If the V-belt pulley on a power saw is too loose, it is MOST likely to cause 17.____

    A. the blade to turn when the engine idles
    B. damage to the clutch bearing
    C. the motor to stall when the blade is stopped
    D. slipping

18. The above passage says that a power saw should never be run without a(n) 18.____

    A. air filter   B. fuel filter
    C. V-belt pulley   D. blade

19. Which of the following blades should be replaced when two or more tips are missing?

    A. Both aluminum oxide and carbide-tipped blades
    B. Carbide-tipped blades *only*
    C. Both silicon carbide and aluminum oxide blades
    D. Silicon carbide blades *only*

20. Which of the following blades should be replaced when worn down to an eight-inch diameter or less?

    A. Both aluminum oxide and carbide-tipped blades
    B. Carbide-tipped blades *only*
    C. Both silicon carbide and aluminum oxide blades
    D. Silicon carbide blades *only*

21. Fire engines use diesel motors to make them run. Diesel motors have devices called air cleaners which keep dirt from the inside of the motor. To make sure that the air cleaners are cleaned or replaced when necessary, an indicator on the fire engine will display a red color if the air cleaner has become too dirty. Each time the lubricating oil in the motor is changed, or whenever the indicator shows red, the air cleaners must be inspected and cleaned or replaced.
    Of the following, the MOST accurate statement concerning air cleaners on fire engine diesel motors is that they should be

    A. cleaned every day
    B. replaced only when the oil is changed
    C. inspected and cleaned only when the oil is changed
    D. inspected and cleaned or replaced when the indicator shows red

22. Firefighter Green must check the supply of air tank cylinders at the beginning of each tour of duty. There must be ten air tank cylinders always full of air and ready to be exchanged for used, empty air tank cylinders. At the start of a new tour of duty, Firefighter Green finds that out of twenty cylinders present, only five cylinders are full and ready to be exchanged.
    What is the MINIMUM number of used empty cylinders that Firefighter Green must replace with full cylinders?

    A. 5   B. 10   C. 15   D. 20

Questions 23-25.

DIRECTIONS: Questions 23 through 25 are to be answered SOLELY on the basis of the following passage.

Automatic sprinkler systems are installed in many buildings. They extinguish or keep from spreading 96% of all fires in areas they protect. Sprinkler systems are made up of pipes which hang below the ceiling of each protected area and sprinkler heads which are placed along the pipes. The pipes are usually filled with water, and each sprinkler head has a heat sensitive part. When the heat from the fire reaches the sensitive part of the sprinkler head, the head opens and showers water upon the fire in the form of spray. The heads are spaced so that the fire is covered by overlapping showers of water from the open heads.

23. Automatic sprinkler systems are installed in buildings to

    A. prevent the build-up of dangerous gases
    B. eliminate the need for fire insurance
    C. extinguish fires or keep them from spreading
    D. protect 96% of the floor space

24. If more than one sprinkler head opens, the area sprayed will be

    A. flooded with hot water
    B. overlapped by showers of water
    C. subject to less water damage
    D. about 1 foot per sprinkler head

25. A sprinkler head will open and shower water when

    A. it is reached by heat from a fire
    B. water pressure in the pipes gets too high
    C. it is reached by sounds from a fire alarm
    D. water temperature in the pipes gets too low

KEY (CORRECT ANSWERS)

1.	B	11.	B
2.	B	12.	D
3.	C	13.	A
4.	A	14.	B
5.	D	15.	D
6.	D	16.	C
7.	D	17.	D
8.	C	18.	A
9.	B	19.	B
10.	C	20.	C

21. D
22. A
23. C
24. B
25. A

FIRE SCIENCE

EXAMINATION SECTION
TEST 1

Questions 1-10.   Booklet/Floor Plan

Firefighters must be able to find their way in and out of buildings that are filled with smoke. They must learn the floor plan quickly for their own safety and to help fight the fire and remove victims.

Look at this floor plan of an apartment. There is an apartment on each side of this one. It is on the fifth floor of the building.

Doors are shown as

Doorways are shown as

windows are shown as

You will have 5 minutes to memorize this floor plan. Then you will be asked to answer some questions about it without looking at it.

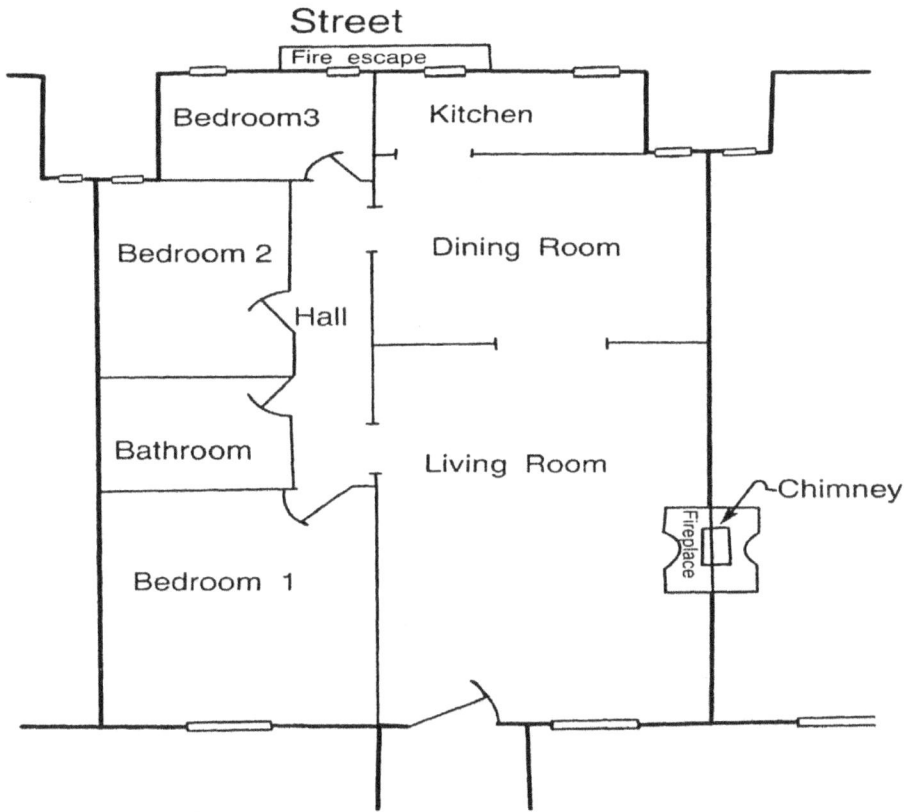

Questions 1-10.   Visual Recall

DIRECTIONS: Questions 1 through 10 test your ability to recall the details of the floor plan you have just studied. Each question or statement is followed by four choices. For each question, choose the one BEST answer (A, B, C, or D). Then *PRINT THE LETTER OF THE CORRECT ANSWER IN THE SPACE AT THE RIGHT.*

1. Which room has NO doors that can be closed?

    A. Bedroom 1
    B. Living room
    C. Dining room
    D. None of these

2. Which room is FARTHEST from the bathroom?

    A. Bedroom 3
    B. Living room
    C. Dining room
    D. Kitchen

3. If there is a fire in the living room, firefighters entering from the fire escape should bring a hose in through

    A. the kitchen window
    B. the hall
    C. the window of bedroom 2
    D. any one of the above

4. It would be MOST important to check for a fire in the apartment next door if a fire in this apartment were in

    A. the kitchen
    B. bedroom 3
    C. the hall
    D. the chimney above the fireplace

5. If a firefighter were rescuing a person in bedroom 2 and the fire were in bedroom 3, the *safest* way of escape would be through the

    A. window of bedroom 2
    B. hall and living room
    C. kitchen to the fire escape
    D. hall to dining room window

6. Which room has *only one* way of escaping from it?

    A. The bathroom
    B. The living room
    C. Bedroom 2
    D. None of the above

7. If the hall were full of fire and heavy smoke, a ladder would be necessary to remove a person trapped in

    A. the dining room
    B. the kitchen
    C. the living room
    D. bedroom

8. Which room has *four* ways of escape?

    A. Bedroom 1   B. Diningroom   C. Kitchen   D. None of them

9. Which room does NOT have a door or doorway leading directly into the hall?

    A. The bathroom
    B. The living room
    C. The kitchen
    D. Bedroom 1

10. Of the following, the SHORTEST way from the fire escape to the kitchen is through   10._____
    A. bedroom 3, hall, and dining room
    B. bedroom 2, hall, and dining room
    C. bedroom 1, living room, and dining room
    D. the living room and dining room

KEY (CORRECT ANSWERS)

1. C
2. D
3. A
4. D
5. B

6. A
7. D
8. B
9. C
10. A

READING COMPREHENSION

UNDERSTANDING WRITTEN MATERIALS

EXAMINATION SECTION

DIRECTIONS FOR THIS SECTION:

Each question or incomplete statement is followed by several suggested answers or completions. Select the one that *BEST* answers the question or completes the statement. *THEN, PRINT THE LETTER OF THE CORRECT ANSWER IN THE SPACE AT THE RIGHT.*

Your answers are to be based *ONLY* on the information that is given or that can be assumed from the reading passages.

TEST 1

Questions 1-5.

DIRECTIONS: Answer Questions 1 through 5 on' the basis of the passage below.

Arsonists are people who set fires deliberately, They don't look like criminals, but they cost the nation millions of dollars in property loss, and sometimes loss of life. Arsonists set fires for many different reasons. Sometimes a shopkeeper sees no way out of losing his business, and sets fire to it so he can collect the insurance. Another type of arsonist wants revenge, and sets fire to the home or shop of someone he feels has treated him unfairly. Some arsonists just like the excitement of seeing the fire burn and watching the firefighters at work; arsonists of this type have even been known to help fight the fire.

1. The writer of the passage feels that arsonists
    A. usually return to the scene of the crime
    B. work at night   C. don't look like criminals
    D. never leave their fingerprints

2. An arsonist is a person who
    A. intentionally sets a fire   B. enjoys watching fires
    C. wants revenge   D. needs money

3. Arsonists have been known to help fight fires because they
    A. felt guilty   B. enjoyed the excitement
    C. wanted to earn money   D. didn't want anyone hurt

4. Shopkeepers sometimes become arsonists in order to
    A. commit suicide   B. collect insurance money
    C. hide a crime   D. raise their prices

5. The *point* of this passage is that arsonists
    A. would make good firefighters   B. are not criminals
    C. are mentally ill   D. are not all alike

Questions 6-11.

DIRECTIONS: Answer Questions 6 through 11 on the basis of the passage below.

Water and ventilation are the keys to fire fighting. Firefighters put out most fires by hosing water on the burning material, and by letting the smoke and gases out. When burning material is soaked with cooling water it can no longer produce gases that burn. In a closed room, hot gases can raise the temperature enough for the room to burst into flame. This can happen even though the room is far away from the fire itself. Therefore, firefighters chop holes in roofs and smash windows in order to empty the house of gases quickly. This is called ventilation.

6. Burning material will stop giving off hot gases when it is 6._____
   A. allowed to burn freely   B. exposed to fresh air
   C. cooled with water   D. sprayed with chemicals

7. Hot gases cause a room to burn by 7._____
   A. creating a draft   B. exploding
   C. giving off sparks   D. raising the room temperature

8. A room can burst into flames even though it is 8._____
   A. far from the fire   B. soaked with water
   C. well ventilated   D. cold and damp

9. Firefighters sometimes smash windows and chop holes in roofs in order to 9._____
   A. reach trapped victims   B. remove burning materials
   C. ventilate a building   D. escape from a fire

10. Ventilation is important in fire fighting because it 10._____
   A. releases trapped smoke and gases
   B. puts out flames by cooling them
   C. makes it easier for firefighters to breathe
   D. makes the flames easier to see and reach with a hose

11. Hot gases are *most* dangerous when they are in a room that is 11._____
   A. large   B. closed   C. damp   D. cool

Questions 12-15.

DIRECTIONS: Answer Questions 12 through 15 on the basis of the passage below.

When there is a large fire in an occupied apartment or tenement, the fire escapes often become overcrowded. To relieve this overcrowding, a portable ladder is often raised to the first level of the fire escape and put opposite to the drop ladder. For added help, an additional ladder can be raised from the ground to the second level. If the fire escape is located in the rear of the building, a "gooseneck" ladder that hooks over the roof can also be used. Then firefighters can help some occupants from the fire escape to the roof instead of to the ground.

12. Portable ladders are raised to fire escapes so that 12._____
    A. firefighters can reach the roof from outside
    B. occupants can reach a higher level of the fire escape
    C. firefighters can enter windows more easily
    D. occupants can leave fire escapes more rapidly

13. If all the ladders described in the passage are used, *how many* ways can the 13._____
    occupants reach the ground directly by ladder from the fire escape at the first
    level?
    A. 1   B. 2   C. 3   D. 4

14. A "gooseneck" ladder is sometimes used 14._____
    A. opposite the drop ladder   B. from the top level
    C. from the first level   D. from the second level

15. The *main* topic of the paragraph is: 15._____
    A. Relieving overcrowding on fire escapes
    B. Setting up and using portable ladders
    C. Rescuing occupants from apartments
    D. Using the roof to escape from fires

Questions 16-20.

DIRECTIONS: Answer Questions 16 through 20 on the basis of the passage below.

Fire often travels inside the partitions of a burning building. Many partitions contain wooden studs that support the partitions. The studs leave a space for the fire to travel along. Flames may spread from the bottom to the upper floors through the partitions. Sparks from a fire in the upper part of a partition may fall and start a fire at the bottom. Some signs that a fire is spreading inside a partition are: (1) blistering paint, (2) discolored paint or wallpaper, or (3) partitions that feel hot to the touch. If any of these signs is present, the partition must be opened up to look for the fire. Finding cobwebs inside the partition is one sign that fire has not spread through the partition.

16. Fires can spread inside partitions because 16._____
    A. there are spaces between studs inside of partitions
    B. fires can burn anywhere
    C. partitions are made out of materials that burn easily
    D. partitions are usually painted or wallpapered

17. Cobwebs inside a partition are a sign that the fire has not spread inside the 17._____
    partition because
    A.. cobwebs are fire resistant
    B. fire destroys cobwebs easily
    C. spiders don't build cobwebs near fires
    D. cobwebs fill up the spaces between studs

18. If a firefighter sees the paint on a partition beginning to blister, he should *first* 18._____
    A. wet down the partition
    B. check the partitions in other rooms
    C. chop a hole in the partition
    D. close windows and doors and leave the room

19. *One* way to tell if fire is spreading within a partition is the
    A. temperature of the partition   B. color of the smoke
    C. age of the plaster   D. spacing of the studs

20. The *main* point of the passage is:
    A. How fire spreads inside partitions
    B. How cobwebs help firefighters
    C. How partitions are built
    D. How to keep fires from spreading

Questions 21-25.

DIRECTIONS: Answer Questions 21 through 25 on the basis of the passage below.

There is hardly a city in the country that is not short of fire protection in some areas within its boundaries. These municipalities have spread out and have re-shuffled their residential, business, and industrial districts without readjusting the existing protective fire forces, or creating new protection units. Fire stations are still situated according to the needs of earlier times and have not been altered or improved to house modern fire fighting equipment. They are neither efficient for carrying out their tasks nor livable for the men who must occupy them.

21. Of the following, the title which *BEST* describes the central idea of the above passage is:
    A. The Dynamic Nature of Contemporary Society
    B. The Cost of Fire Protection
    C. The Location and Design of Fire Stations
    D. The Design and Use of Fire Fighting Equipment
    E. The Growth of American Cities

22. According to the above passage, fire protection is inadequate in the United States in
    A. *most* areas of *some* cities
    B. *some* areas of *most* cities
    C. *some* areas in *all* cities
    D. *all* areas in *some* cities
    E. *most* areas in *most* cities

23. The *one* of the following criteria for planning of fire stations which is *NOT* mentioned in the above passage is:
    A. Comfort of firemen   B. Proper location
    C. Design for modern equipment
    D. Efficiency of operation   E. Cost of construction

24. Of the following suggestions for improving the fire service, the *one* which would *BEST* deal with the problem discussed in the passage above would involve
    A. specialized training in the use of modern fire apparatus
    B. replacement of obsolete fire apparatus
    C. revision of zoning laws
    D. longer basic training for probationary firemen
    E. reassignment of fire districts

25. The tone of the author of the passage above may BEST be characterized by 25._____
which one of the following adjectives:
A. Hopeful   B. Negative   C. Hopeless   D. Striving   E. Critical

TEST 2

Questions 1-6.

DIRECTIONS: Answer Questions 1 through 6 on the basis of the passage below.

During search operations the first step is usually to rescue victims who can be seen and heard, or those whose exact locations are known. Disorganized or careless search must be avoided since victims may be underneath rubble. Disorganized movement could cause injury or death. The best method is to start from the outer edge and work toward the center of an area. Sometimes a trapped or buried victim may be located by calling out or by tapping on pipes. Rescue workers should first call out, then have a period of silence to listen for sounds from a victim.

1. The *main* point of the paragraph is that 1._____
   A. firefighters should call and listen often
   B. trapped victims can usually be heard
   C. searching should be an organized procedure
   D. many victims are buried in fires

2. Normally, the *first* victims to be rescued during a search are those who are 2._____
   A. unconscious   B. trapped under rubble
   C. easy to see and hear   D. injured

3. When searching for buried victims, it is very important for firefighters to 3._____
   A. have periods of silence   B. keep moving constantly
   C. search rubble piles quickly
   D. stay away from rubble piles

4. The *best* way to search an area is 4._____
   A. around the edges   B. from center to edge
   C. from corner to corner   D. from edge to center

5. Disorganized movement by a rescue worker can cause 5._____
   A. panic and confusion   B. property destruction
   C. wasted time   D. death or injury

6. Tapping on pipes is a good way to locate victims because 6._____
   A. firefighters can use Morse code
   B. sound travels through a pipe
   C. firefighters can signal each other this way
   D. pipes usually aren't covered by rubble

Questions 7-10.

DIRECTIONS: Answer Questions 7 through 10 on the basis of the passage below.

When backing a fire truck into the firehouse, all firefighters should remain outside the building. Firefighters assigned to stop traffic should face traffic so they can alert the driver in case of an emergency. Additional firefighters should stand on the sidewalk in front of the firehouse to guide the driver. The truck should be slowly backed into the firehouse and immediately stopped upon orders of any firefighter. When the truck is completely in the firehouse, then and only then should the officer contact central headquarters for the placement of the company in service. Following this, the officer orders the entrance doors closed.

Use this diagram to help answer Questions 7 through 9. The letters indicate where firefighters are standing.

7. The truck is backing into the firehouse. *Which* firefighter is *NOT* needed according to the regulations?
   A. Firefighter A
   B. Firefighter B
   C. Firefighter C
   D. Firefighter D

8. *Which* firefighters are responsible for stopping cars? Firefighters
   A. A and C   B. C and E   C. A and B   D. B and E

9. *Which* firefighters can order the truck to stop?
   A. Firefighters A and B only
   B. Firefighters C and E only
   C. Firefighter D only
   D. Any of them

10. When is central headquarters notified that the company is ready to be put in service? 10.____
   A. When the truck is returning from a fire
   B. After the truck is parked in the firehouse
   C. After the firehouse doors are closed
   D. When all of the firefighters have entered the firehouse

Questions 11-15.

DIRECTIONS: Answer Questions 11 through 15 on the basis of the passage below.

Unless they have had a fire, most people are not aware of the things firefighters do. Too often the public thinks of firefighters as lounging around a firehouse between fires. Firefighters can help change this image in small ways by their appearance, by greeting visitors who come to the firehouse, by their behavior on the street at a fire, and by treating the public in a courteous manner. For example, 90 percent of the rescues made by the average fire department take place at relatively small fires, not at spectacular extra alarm fires. The public rarely hears about them because the fire departments seldom let the press know about firefighters who have performed acts of bravery at routine fires.

11. *What* are firefighters doing when not fighting fires? 11.____
    A. Lounging around the firehouse
    B. Working on public relations projects
    C. Making repairs to the equipment
    D. The passage doesn't say

12. The passage places responsibility for improving the fire department's image on the 12.____
    A. fire department itself   B. press   C. public
    D. people rescued by firefighters

13. *Most* of the rescues made by firefighters take place at 13.____
    A. extra alarm fires
    B. special emergencies where no fire is involved
    C. relatively small fires   D. spectacularly large fires

14. The public rarely hears about rescues made by firefighters at routine fires because 14.____
    A. information about fires must be kept confidential
    B. fire departments seldom report these rescues to the press
    C. most of these rescues take place late at night
    D. reporters aren't interested in covering routine fires

15. *What* would be the *BEST* title for this passage? 15.____
    A. An Inside Look at the Fire Department
    B. Making the Most of Fire Prevention Week
    C. Improving the Fire Department's Public Image
    D. Brave Acts Performed by Firefighters

Questions 16-19.

DIRECTIONS: Answer Questions 16 through 19 on the basis of the passage below.

Ventilation, as used in fire-fighting operations, means opening up a building or structure in which a fire is burning to release the accumulated heat, smoke and gases. Lack of knowledge of the principles of ventilation on the part of firemen may result in unnecessary punishment due to ventilation being neglected or improperly handled. While ventilation itself extinguishes no fires, when used in an intelligent manner, it allows firemen to get at the fire more quickly, easily, and with less danger and hardship.

16. According to the above paragraph, the *MOST* important result of failure to apply the principles of ventilation at a fire may be   16._____
    A. loss of public confidence   B. disciplinary action
    C. waste of water   D. excessive use of equipment
    E. injury to firemen

17. It may be inferred from the above paragraph that the *CHIEF* advantage of ventilation is that it   17._____
    A. eliminates the need for gas masks
    B. reduces smoke damage
    C. permits firemen to work closer to the fire
    D. cools the fire
    E. enables firemen to use shorter hose lines

18. Knowledge of the principles of ventilation, as defined in the above paragraph, would be *LEAST* important in a fire in a   18._____
    A. tenement house   B. grocery store   C. ship's hold
    D. lumberyard   E. office building

19. We may conclude from the above paragraph that, for the well-trained and equipped fireman, ventilation is   19._____
    A. a simple matter   B. rarely necessary
    C. relatively unimportant   D. a basic tool
    E. sometimes a handicap

Questions 20-22.

DIRECTIONS: Answer Questions 20 through 22 on the basis of the passage below.

A fire of undetermined origin started in the warehouse shed of a flour mill. Although there was some delay in notifying the fire department, they practically succeeded in bringing the fire under control when a series of dust explosions occurred which caused the fire to spread and the main building was destroyed. The fire department's efforts were considerably handicapped because it was undermanned, and the water pressure in the vicinity was inadequate.

20. From the information contained in the above paragraph, it is *MOST* accurate to state that the cause of the fire was   20._____
    A. suspicious   B. unknown   C. accidental
    D. arson   E. spontaneous combustion

21. In the fire described above, the MOST important cause of the fire spreading to the main building was the 21._____
    A. series of dust explosions
    B. delay in notifying the fire department
    C. inadequate water pressure
    D. lack of manpower
    E. wooden construction of the building

22. In the fire described above, the fire department's efforts were handicapped CHIEFLY by 22._____
    A. poor leadership
    B. out-dated apparatus
    C. uncooperative company employees
    D. insufficient water pressure   E. poorly trained men

Questions 23-25.

DIRECTIONS: Answer Questions 23 through 25 on the basis of the passage below.

A flameproof fabric is defined as one which, when exposed to small sources of ignition such as sparks or smoldering cigarettes, does not burn beyond the vicinity of the source of the ignition. Cotton fabrics are the materials commonly used that are considered most hazardous. Other materials, such as acetate rayons and linens, are somewhat less hazardous, and woolens and some natural silk fabrics, even when untreated, are about the equal of the average treated cotton fabric insofar as flame-spread and ease of ignition are concerned. The method of application is to immerse the fabric in a flameproofing solution. The container used must be large enough so that all the fabric is thoroughly wet and there are no folds which the solution does not penetrate.

23. According to the above paragraph, a flameproof fabric is one which 23._____
    A. is unaffected by heat and smoke
    B. resists the spread of flames when ignited
    C. burns with a cold flame
    D. cannot be ignited by sparks or cigarettes
    E. may smolder but cannot burn

24. According to the above paragraph, woolen fabrics which have not been flameproofed are as likely to catch fire as 24._____
    A. treated silk fabrics
    B. treated acetate rayon fabrics
    C. untreated linen fabrics
    D. untreated synthetic fabrics
    E. treated cotton fabrics

25. In the method described above, the flameproofing solution is BEST applied to the fabric by 25._____
    A. sponging the fabric   B. spraying the fabric
    C. dipping the fabric   D. brushing the fabric
    E. sprinkling the fabric

KEYS (CORRECT ANSWER)

TEST 1		TEST 2	
1. C	11. B	1. C	11. D
2. A	12. D	2. C	12. A
3. B	13. B	3. A	13. C
4. B	14. B	4. D	14. B
5. D	15. A	5. D	15. C
6. C	16. A	6. B	16. E
7. D	17. B	7. D	17. C
8. A	18. C	8. C	18. D
9. C	19. A	9. D	19. D
10. A	20. A	10. B	20. B
21. C		21. A	
22. B		22. D	
23. E		23. B	
24. E		24. E	
25. E		25. C	

READING COMPREHENSION
UNDERSTANDING AND INTERPRETING WRITTEN MATERIAL

EXAMINATION SECTION
TEST 1

DIRECTIONS: Each question or incomplete statement is followed by several suggested answers or completions. Select the one that BEST answers the question or completes the statement. *PRINT THE LETTER OF THE COREECT ANSWER IN THE SPACE AT THE RIGHT.*

Questions 1-3.

DIRECTIONS: Questions 1 through 3 are to be answered SOLELY on the basis of the following paragraph.

When wood products are heated sufficiently under fire conditions, they undergo thermal decomposition and evolve various combustible gases or vapors which burn as the familiar flames. After these volatile decomposition products of the wood are driven off, the combustible residue is essentially carbon which on further heating undergoes surface combustion reactions with the oxygen of the air, producing considerable heat (glowing), but usually very little flame.

1. The one of the following explanations of thermal decomposition that is MOST accurate is that it is a process by which 1.____

   A. heat is transferred from solid substances to gaseous substances
   B. a substance is consumed during the course of a fire
   C. a substance is broken down into component parts when subjected to heat
   D. heat is generated until the ignition point of the substance is reached

2. The one of the following statements that is MOST accurate is that pure carbon has an ignition temperature which, compared to the combustible vapors of wood, is 2.____

   A. lower
   B. approximately the same
   C. higher
   D. higher or lower, depending upon the variety of wood involved

3. A substance which burns with a large amount of flames is one that 3.____

   A. contains a large amount of inorganic material
   B. produces during the burning process a large amount of pure carbon
   C. contains a large amount of calories per unit of combustibles
   D. produces during the burning process a large amount of combustible gases or vapors

Questions 4-7.

DIRECTIONS: Questions 4 through 7 are to be answered SOLELY on the basis of the following paragraph.

For the five year period 1996-2000, inclusive, the average annual fire loss in the United States amounted to approximately $2,709,760,000. Included in this estimate is $2,045,332,000 damage to buildings and contents, and $564,328,000 average annual loss in aircraft, motor vehicles, forest and other miscellaneous fires not involving buildings. Preliminary estimates indicate that the total United States fire loss in 1981 was $3,230,000,000. These are property damage fire losses only and do not include indirect losses resulting from fires which are just as real and sometimes far more serious than property damage losses. But because evaluation of indirect monetary losses is usually very difficult, their importance in the national fire waste picture is often overlooked.

4. According to the data in the above paragraph, the BEST of the following estimates of the total direct fire loss in the United States for the six year period 1996-2001, inclusive, is

    A. $2,800,000,000
    B. $5,400,000,000
    C. $14,000,000,000
    D. $16,800,000,000

5. The BEST example of an indirect fire loss, as that term is used in the above paragraph, is monetary loss due to

    A. smoke or water damage to exposures
    B. condemnation of foodstuffs following a fire
    C. interruption of business following a fire
    D. forcible entry by firemen operating at a fire

6. Suppose that during the period 2001-2005 the average annual fire loss to buildings and contents increases 10 percent and the average annual loss due to fires not involving buildings decreases 10 percent.
The MOST valid of the following conclusions is that the average annual fire loss for the 2001-2005 period, compared to the losses for the 1996-2000 period,

    A. will increase
    B. will decrease
    C. will be unchanged
    D. cannot be calculated from the information given

7. If a comparison is made between total annual direct and indirect fire losses on the basis of the information given in the above paragraph, the MOST valid of the following conclusions is that

    A. generally direct losses are higher
    B. generally indirect losses are higher
    C. generally direct and indirect losses are approximately equal
    D. there is not sufficient information to determine which is higher or if they are approximately equal

Questions 8-10.

DIRECTIONS: Questions 8 through 10 are to be answered SOLELY on the basis of the following paragraph.

The soda-acid fire extinguisher is the commonest type of water solution extinguisher in which pressure is used to expel the water. The chemicals used are sodium bicarbonate (baking soda) and sulfuric acid. The sodium bicarbonate is dissolved in water, and this solution is the extinguishing agent. The extinguishing value of the stream is that of an equal quantity of water.

8. According to the above paragraph, the soda-acid extinguisher, compared to others of the same type, is the   8._____

   A. most widely used
   B. most effective in putting out fire
   C. cheapest to operate
   D. easiest to operate

9. In the soda-acid extinguisher, the fire is put out by a solution of sodium bicarbonate and   9._____

   A. sulfuric acid   B. baking soda
   C. soda-acid   D. water

10. According to the above paragraph, the sodium bicarbonate solution, compared to water, is   10._____

    A. *more* effective in putting out fires
    B. *less* effective in putting out fires
    C. *equally* effective in putting out fires
    D. *more* or *less* effective, depending upon the type of fire

Questions 11-13.

DIRECTIONS: Questions 11 through 13 are to be answered SOLELY on the basis of the following paragraph.

The average daily flow of water through public water systems in American cities ranges generally between 40 and 250 gallons per capita, depending upon the underground leakage in the system, the amount of waste in domestic premises, and the qua.ntity used for industrial purposes. The problem of supplying this water has become serious in many cities. Supplies, once adequate, in many cases have become seriously deficient, due to greater demands with increased population and growing industrial use of water. Water works, operating on fixed schedules of water charges, have in many cases not been able to afford the heavy capital expenditures necessary to provide adequate supply, storage, and distribution facilities. Thus, the adequacy of a public water supply for fire protection in any given location cannot properly be taken for granted.

11. The four programs listed below are possible ways by which American communities might try to reduce the seriousness of the water shortage problem.   11._____
    The one of the four programs which does NOT directly follow from the paragraph above is the program of

    A. regular replacement of old street water mains by new ones
    B. inspection and repair of leaky plumbing fixtures
    C. fire prevention inspection and education to reduce the amount of water used to extinguish fires
    D. research into industrial processes to reduce the amount of water used in those processes

12. The MAIN conclusion reached by the author of the above paragraph is

    A. there is a waste of precious natural resources in America
    B. communities have failed to control the industrial use of water
    C. a need exists for increasing the revenue of water works to build up adequate supplies of water
    D. fire departments cannot assume that they will always have the necessary supply of water available to fight fires

13. Per capita consumption of water of a community is determined by the formula

    A. $\dfrac{\text{Population}}{\text{Total consumption in gallons}} = \text{per capita consumption in gallons}$

    B. $\dfrac{\text{Total consumption in gallons}}{\text{Population}} = \text{per capita consumption in gallons}$

    C. Total consumption in gallons x population = per capita consumption in gallons
    D. Total consumption in gallons - population = Per capita consumption in gallons

Questions 14-17.

DIRECTIONS: Questions 14 through 17 are to be answered SOLELY on the basis of the following paragraph.

Language performs an essentially social function; it helps us to get along together, to communicate and achieve a great measure of concerted action. Words are signs which have significance by convention, and those people who do not adopt the conventions simply fail to communicate. They do not *get along* and a social force arises which encourages them to achieve the correct associations. *Correct* means as used by other members of the social group. Some of the vital points about language are brought home to an Englishman when visiting America, and vice versa, because our vocabularies are nearly the same — but not quite.

14. *Communicate*, as that word is used in the above paragraph, means to

    A. make ourselves understood
    B. send written messages
    C. move other persons to concerted action
    D. use language in its traditional or conventional sense

15. Usage of a word is *correct*, as that term is defined in the above paragraph, when the word is used as it is

    A. defined in standard dictionaries
    B. used by the majority of persons throughout the world who speak the same language
    C. used by the majority of educated persons who speak the same language
    D. used by other persons with whom we are associating

16. In the above paragraph, the author is concerned PRIMARILY with the 16._____
    A. meaning of words
    B. pronunciation of words
    C. structure of sentences
    D. origin and development of language

17. According to the above paragraph, the MAIN language problem of an Englishman, while 17._____
    visiting America, stems from the fact that an Englishman
    A. uses some words that have different meanings for Americans
    B. has different social values than the Americans
    C. has had more exposure to non-English speaking persons than Americans have had
    D. pronounces words differently than Americans do

Questions 18-21.

DIRECTIONS: Questions 18 through 21 are to be answered SOLELY on the basis of the following paragraph.

Whenever a social group has become so efficiently organized that it has gained access to an adequate supply of food and has learned to distribute it among its members so well that wealth considerably exceeds immediate demands, it can be depended upon to utilize its surplus energy in an attempt to enlarge the sphere in which it is active. The structure of ant colonies renders them particularly prone to this sort of expansionist policy. With very few exceptions, ants of any given colony are hostile to those of any other community, even of the same species, and this condition is bound to produce preliminary bickering among colonies which are closely associated.

18. According to the above paragraph, a social group is wealthy when it 18._____
    A. is efficiently organized
    B. controls large territories
    C. contains energetic members
    D. produces and distributes food reserves

19. According to the above paragraph, the structure of an ant colony is its 19._____
    A. social organization   B. nest arrangement
    C. territorial extent   D. food-gathering activities

20. It follows from the above paragraph that the LEAST expansionist society would be one 20._____
    that has
    A. great poverty generally
    B. more than sufficient wealth to meet its immediate demands
    C. great wealth generally
    D. wide inequality between its richest and poorest members

21. According to the above paragraph, an ant generally is hostile EXCEPT to other   21._____
    A. insects
    B. ants
    C. ants of the same species
    D. ants of the same colony

Questions 22-25.

DIRECTIONS: Questions 22 through 25 are to be answered SOLELY on the basis of the following paragraph.

Steel used in boiler construction must be of a higher quality than steel used in general construction. The boiler steel must be capable of sustaining loads at elevated temperatures. Temperature has a more serious effect upon the boiler fabrication than has the pressure. The material for bolts and studs is conditioned by tempering. The tempering temperature is at least 100F higher than the service operating temperature. All materials used in boiler construction must be creep resistant to minimize the relaxation in service. Fire box quality plate is used for any part of a boiler exposed to the fire or products of combustion. For parts of the boiler subject to pressure and not exposed to fire or products of combustion, flange quality plate is used. A small percentage of molybdenum is added to steel in the manufacture of superheater tubes, piping, and valves to increase the ability of these parts to withstand high temperature.

22. Material for bolts and studs used on boilers is conditioned for service by   22._____
    A. tempering   B. re-tightening
    C. forging   D. anodizing

23. The part of a boiler that is exposed to products of combustion is made of   23._____
    A. alloy materials   B. firebox quality plate
    C. flange quality plate   D. carbon steel

24. Temperature has a MORE serious effect upon boiler fabrication than has the   24._____
    A. vibration   B. steam   C. relaxation   D. pressure

25. When comparing steel used in boiler construction to steel used in general construction, it can be said that steel used in boiler construction must be of a   25._____
    A. high-weld strength   B. low-carbon content
    C. lower quality   D. higher quality

KEY (CORRECT ANSWERS)

1. C
2. C
3. D
4. D
5. C

6. A
7. D
8. A
9. D
10. C

11. C
12. D
13. B
14. A
15. D

16. A
17. A
18. D
19. A
20. A

21. D
22. A
23. B
24. D
25. D

TEST 2

Questions 1-3.

DIRECTIONS: Questions 1 through 3 are to be answered SOLELY on the basis of the following paragraph.

    A fire of undetermined origin started in the warehouse shed of a flour mill. Although there was some delay in notifying the fire department, they practically succeeded in bringing the fire under control when a series of dust explosions occurred which caused the fire to spread and the main building was destroyed. The fire department's efforts were considerably handicapped because it was undermanned, and the water pressure in the vicinity was inadequate.

1. From the information contained in the above paragraph, it is MOST accurate to state that the cause of the fire was

   A. suspicious
   B. unknown
   C. accidental
   D. spontaneous combustion

2. In the fire described above, the MOST important cause of the fire spreading to the main building was the

   A. series of dust explosions
   B. delay in notifying the fire department
   C. inadequate water pressure
   D. wooden construction of the building

3. In the fire described above, the fire department's efforts were handicapped CHIEFLY by

   A. poor leadership
   B. outdated apparatus
   C. uncooperative company employees
   D. insufficient water pressure

Questions 4-6.

DIRECTIONS: Questions 4 through 6 are to be answered SOLELY on the basis of the following paragraph.

    A flameproof fabric is defined as one which, when exposed to small sources of ignition such as sparks or smoldering cigarettes, does not burn beyond the vicinity of the source of the ignition. Cotton fabrics are the materials commonly used that are considered most hazardous. Other materials, such as acetate rayons and linens, are somewhat less hazardous, and woolens and some natural silk fabrics, even when untreated, are about the equal of the average treated cotton fabric insofar as flame spread and ease of ignition are concerned. The method of application is to immerse the fabric in a flameproofing solution. The container used must be large enough so that all the fabric is thoroughly wet and there are no folds which the solution does not penetrate.

4. According to the above paragraph, a flameproof fabric is one which 4._____

   A. is unaffected by heat and smoke
   B. resists the spread of flames when ignited
   C. cannot be ignited by sparks or cigarettes
   D. may smolder but cannot burn

5. According to the above paragraph, woolen fabrics which have not been flameproofed are as likely to catch fire as 5._____

   A. treated silk fabrics
   B. untreated linen fabrics
   C. untreated synthetic fabrics
   D. treated cotton fabrics

6. In the method described above, the flameproofing solution is BEST applied to the fabric by _____ the fabric. 6._____

   A. sponging   B. spraying   C. dipping   D. brushing

Questions 7-10.

DIRECTIONS: Questions 7 through 10 are to be answered SOLELY on the basis of the following paragraph.

    There is hardly a city in the country that is not short of fire protection in some areas within its boundaries. These municipalities have spread out and have re-shuffled their residential, business, and industrial districts without readjusting the existing protective fire forces or creating new protection units. Fire stations are still situated according to the needs of earlier times and have not been altered or improved to house modern fire fighting equipment. They are neither efficient for carrying out their tasks nor livable for the men who must occupy them.

7. Of the following, the title which BEST describes the central idea of the above paragraph is 7._____

   A. THE DYNAMIC NATURE OF CONTEMPORARY SOCIETY
   B. THE COST OF FIRE PROTECTION
   C. THE LOCATION AND DESIGN OF FIRE STATIONS
   D. THE DESIGN AND USE OF FIRE FIGHTING EQUIPMENT

8. According to the above paragraph, fire protection is inadequate in the United States in _____ areas _____ cities. 8._____

   A. most; of some   B. some; of most
   C. some; in all   D. most; in most

9. The one of the following criteria for planning of fire stations which is NOT mentioned in the above paragraph is

   A. proper location
   B. design for modern equipment
   C. efficiency of operation
   D. cost of construction

10. Of the following suggestions for improving the fire service, the one which would BEST deal with the problems discussed in the above paragraph would involve

    A. specialized training in the use of modern fire apparatus
    B. replacement of obsolete fire apparatus
    C. longer basic training for probationary firemen
    D. reassignment of fire districts

Questions 11-14.

DIRECTIONS: Questions 11 through 14 are to be answered SOLELY on the basis of the following paragraph.

Gravity tanks for sprinkler systems shall contain an available quantity of water sufficient to supply 25 percent of the number of sprinkler heads in the average protected fire area for twenty minutes, and in any case at least 5,000 gallons. Where there are more than 200 and not more than 400 sprinklers in such average protected fire area, the available quantity of water in excess of 20,000 gallons need not be greater than an amount sufficient to supply 12 1/2 percent of the sprinklers in excess of 200 in such average protected fire area for a period of twenty minutes. If the number of sprinklers in such average fire area exceeds 400, the available quantity of water in excess of 30,000 gallons need not be greater than an amount sufficient to supply six and one-fourth percent of the sprinklers in excess of four hundred in such average protected fire area for a period of twenty minutes.

11. In establishing the required capacity of the gravity tanks for sprinkler systems, the assumption contained in the above paragraph is that the average discharge per minute from sprinkler heads will be _____ gallons.

    A. 20   B. 22   C. 25   D. 28

12. A sprinkler system containing 500 sprinkler heads requires gravity tanks with a minimum capacity of approximately _____ gallons.

    A. 32,500   B. 35,000   C. 37,500   D. 40,000

13. A sprinkler system contains 600 sprinkler heads in the protected fire area. If the minimum requirements of the above paragraph have been met, the gravity tanks should be able to supply for twenty minutes approximately _____ heads.

    A. 88   B. 94   C. 100   D. 106

14. The one of the following graphs which MOST accurately represents the gravity tanks' capacity requirements for sprinkler systems built in accordance with the requirements of the above paragraph is

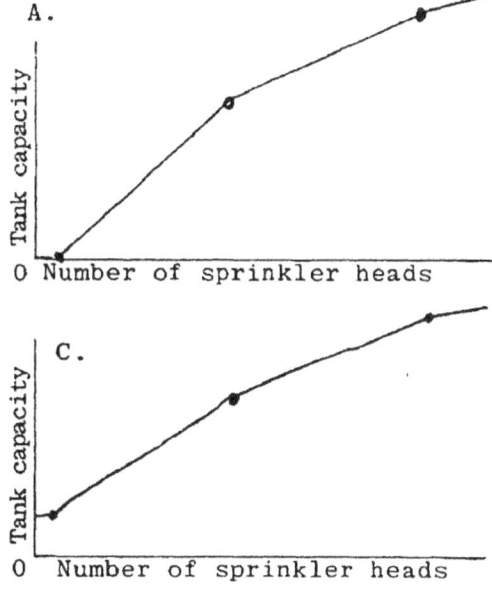
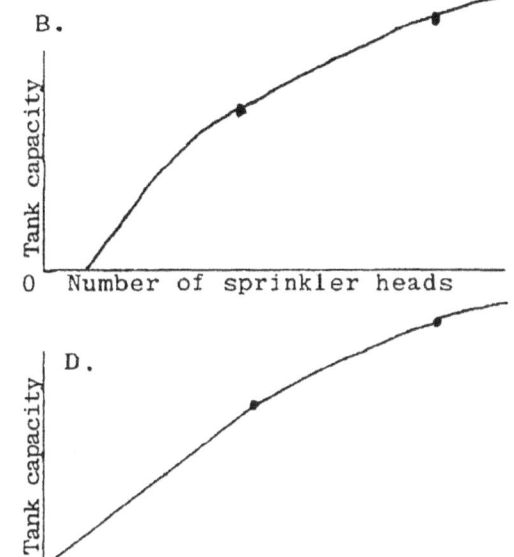

Questions 15-18.

DIRECTIONS: Questions 15 through 18 are to be answered SOLELY on the basis of the following paragraph.

A mixture of a combustible vapor and air will burn only when the proportion of fuel to air lies within a certain range, i.e., between the upper and lower limits of flammability. If a third, non-combustible gas is now added to the mixture, the limits will be narrowed. As increasing amounts of diluent are added, the limits come closer until, at a certain critical concentration, they will converge. This is the peak concentration. It is the minimum amount of diluent that will inhibit the combustion of any fuel-air mixture.

15. If additional diluent is added beyond the peak concentration, the flammable limits of the mixture will

    A. converge rapidly
    B. diverge slowly
    C. diverge rapidly
    D. not be affected

16. If the four numbers listed below were peak concentration values obtained in a test of four diluents, then the MOST efficient diluent would have the value of

    A. 7.5   B. 10   C. 12.5   D. 15

17. The word *inhibit,* as used in the last sentence of the above paragraph, means MOST NEARLY

    A. slow the rate of
    B. prevent entirely the occurrence of
    C. reduce the intensity of
    D. retard to an appreciable extent the manifestation of

18. The one of the graphs below which BEST represents the process described in the above paragraph is

18.____

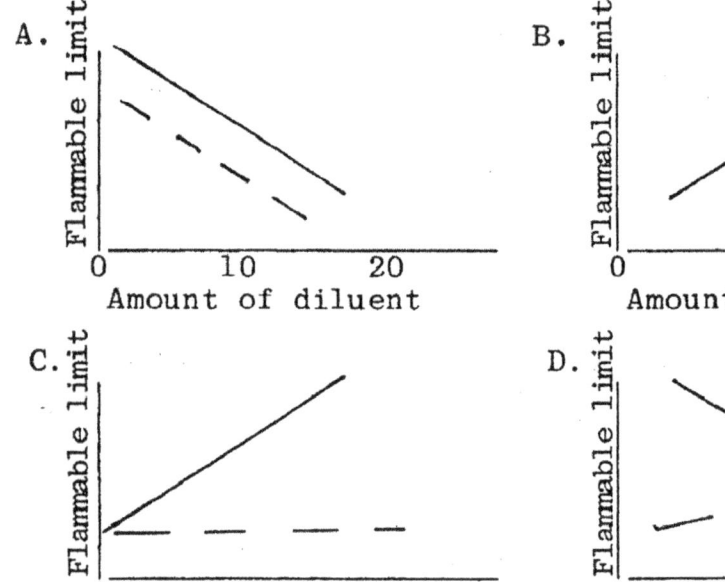

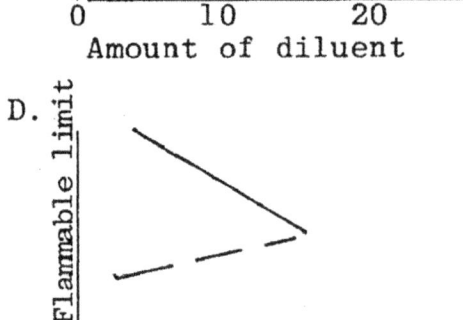

———————— Upper flammable limits
- - - - - - - - - - - Lower flammable limits

Questions 19-22.

DIRECTIONS: Questions 19 through 22 are to be answered SOLELY on the basis of the following paragraph.

The unadjusted loss per $1000 valuation has only a very limited usefulness in evaluating the efficiency of a fire department, for it depends upon the assumption that other factors will remain constant from time to time and city to city. It might be expected that high fire department operation expenditures would tend to be associated with a low fire loss. A statistical study of the loss and cost data in more than 100 cities failed to reveal any such correlation. The lack of relationship, although to some extent due to failure to make the most efficacious expenditure of fire protection funds, must be attributed in part at least to the obscuring effect of variations in the natural, physical, and moral factors which affect fire risk.

19. One reason for the failure to obtain the expected relationship between fire department expenditures and fire loss data which is stated in the above paragraph is the

19.____

A. changing dollar valuation of property
B. unsettling effects of rapid technological innovations
C. inefficiency of some fire department activities
D. statistical errors made by the investigators

20. We may conclude that *the unadjusted loss per $1000* figure is useful in comparing the fire departments of two cities   20.____

    A. only if the cities are of comparable size
    B. only if adjustments are made for other factors which affect fire loss
    C. under no circumstances
    D. only if properly controlled experimental conditions can be obtained

21. The one of the following factors which affect fire risk that is MOST adequately reflected in the *unadjusted loss per $1000 valuation* index is   21.____

    A. fire department operation expenditures
    B. physical characteristics of the city
    C. type of structures most prevalent in the city
    D. total worth of property in the city

22. According to the above paragraph, cities which spend larger sums on their fire departments   22.____

    A. tend to have lower fire losses than cities which spend smaller sums on their fire departments
    B. do not tend to have lower fire losses than cities which spend smaller sums on their fire departments
    C. tend to have higher fire losses than cities which spend smaller sums on their fire departments
    D. do not tend to have the same total property valuation as cities which spend smaller sums on their fire departments

Questions 23-25.

DIRECTIONS: Questions 23 through 25 are to be answered SOLELY on the basis of the following paragraph.

Shafts extending into the top story, except those stair shafts where the stairs do not continue to the roof, shall be carried through and at least two feet above the roof. Every shaft extending above the roof, except open shafts and elevator shafts, shall be enclosed at the top with a roof of materials having a fire resistive rating of one hour and a metal skylight covering at least three-quarters of the area of the shaft in the top story, except that skylights over stair shafts shall have an area not less than one-tenth the area of the shaft in the top story, but shall be not less than fifteen square feet in area. Any shaft terminating below the top story of a structure and those stair shafts not required to extend through the roof shall have the top enclosed with materials having the same fire resistive rating as required for the shaft enclosure.

23. The above paragraph states that the elevator shafts which extend into the top story are   23.____

    A. not required to have a skylight but are required to extend at least two feet above the roof
    B. neither required to have a skylight nor to extend above the roof
    C. required to have a skylight covering at least three-quarters of the area of the shaft in the top story and to extend at least two feet above the roof
    D. required to have a skylight covering at least three-quarters of the area of the shaft in the top story but are not required to extend above the roof

24. The one of the following skylights which meets the requirements of the above paragraph is a skylight measuring

   A. 4' x 4' over a stair shaft which, on the top story, measures 20' x 9'
   B. 4 1/2' x 3 1/2' over a pipe shaft which, on the top story, measures 5' x 4'
   C. 2 1/2' x 1 1/2' over a dumbwaiter shaft which, on the top story, measures 2 1/2' x 2 1/2'
   D. 4' x 3' over a stair shaft which, on the top story, measures 15' x 6'

24._____

25. Suppose that in a Class I building a shaft which does not go to the roof is required to have a three-hour fire resistive rating.
In regard to the material enclosing the top of this shaft, the above paragraph

   A. states that a one-hour fire resistive rating is required
   B. states that a three-hour fire resistive rating is required
   C. implies that no fire resistive rating is required
   D. neither states nor implies anything about the fire resistive rating

25._____

KEY (CORRECT ANSWERS)

1. B
2. A
3. D
4. B
5. D

6. C
7. C
8. B
9. D
10. D

11. A
12. A
13. A
14. C
15. D

16. A
17. B
18. D
19. C
20. B

21. D
22. B
23. A
24. B
25. B

MECHANICAL APTITUDE
MECHANICAL COMPREHENSION
EXAMINATION SECTION
TEST 1

DIRECTIONS: Each question or incomplete statement below is followed by several suggested answers or completions. Select the *one* that *BEST* answers the question or completes the statement. *PRINT THE LETTER OF THE CORRECT ANSWER IN THE SPACE AT THE RIGHT.*

Questions 1-3.

DIRECTIONS: Questions 1 to 3 inclusive are based upon the following paragraph.

The only openings permitted in fire partitions except openings for ventilating ducts shall be those required for doors. There shall be but one such door opening unless the provision of additional openings would not exceed, in total width of all doorways, 25 percent of the length of the wall. The minimum distance between openings shall be three feet. The maximum area for such a door opening shall be 80 square feet, except that such openings for the passage of motor trucks may be a maximum of 140 square feet.

1. According to the above paragraph, openings in fire partitions are permitted *only* for

   A. doors
   B. doors and windows
   C. doors and ventilation ducts
   D. doors, windows and ventilation ducts

2. In a fire partition, 22 feet long and 10 feet high, the *MAXIMUM* number of doors, 3 feet wide and 7 feet high, is

   A. 1   B. 2   C. 3   D. 4

3.

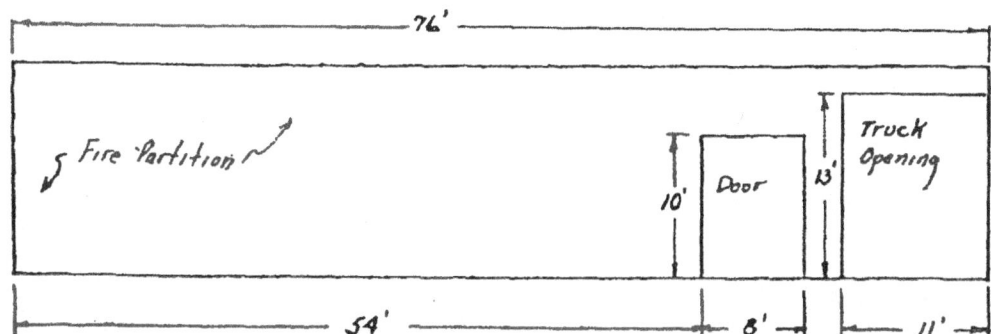

   The one of the following statements about the layout shown above that is *MOST* accurate is that the

   A. total width of the openings is too large
   B. truck opening is too large
   C. truck and door openings are too close together
   D. layout is acceptable

4. At a given temperature, a wet hand will freeze to a bar of metal, but NOT to a piece of wood, because the

    A. metal expands and contracts more than the wood
    B. wood is softer than the metal
    C. wood will burn at a lower temperature than the metal
    D. metal is a better conductor of heat than the wood

5. Of the following items commonly found in a household, the one that uses the MOST electric current is a(n)

    A. 150-watt light bulb
    B. toaster
    C. door buzzer
    D. 8" electric fan

6. Sand and ashes are frequently placed on icy pavements to prevent skidding. The effect of the sand and ashes is to increase

    A. inertia   B. gravity   C. momentum   D. friction

7. The air near the ceiling of a room usually is warmer than the air near the floor because

    A. there is better air circulation at the floor level
    B. warm air is lighter than cold air
    C. windows usually are nearer the floor than the ceiling
    D. heating pipes usually run along the ceiling

8.

DIA. 1   *DIA. 2*

It is safer to use the ladder positioned as shown in diagram 1 than as shown in diagram 2 because, in diagram 1,

    A. less strain is placed upon the center rungs of the ladder
    B. it is easier to grip and stand on the ladder
    C. the ladder reaches a lower height
    D. the ladder is less likely to tip over backwards

9.

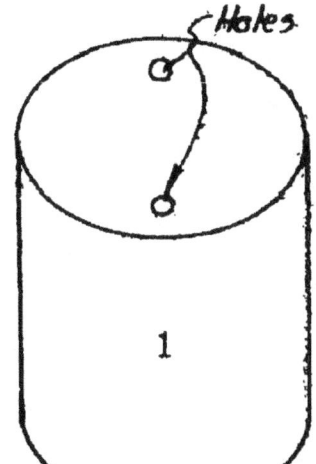
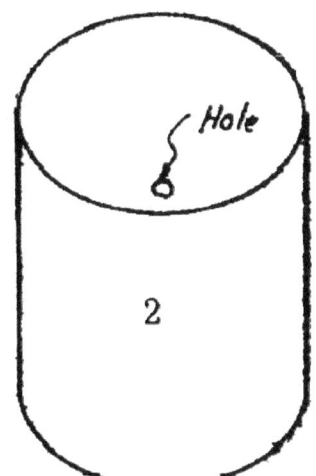

It is *easier* to pour a liquid from:

A. Can 1 because there are two holes from which the liquid can flow
B. Can 1 because air can enter through one hole while the liquid comes out the other hole
C. Can 2 because the liquid comes out under greater pressure
D. Can 2 because it is easier to direct the flow of the liquid when there is only one hole

10. A substance which is subject to "spontaneous combustion" is one that

A. is explosive when heated
B. is capable of catching fire without an external source of heat
C. acts to speed up the burning of material
D. liberates oxygen when heated

11. The sudden shutting down of a nozzle on a hose discharging water under high pressure is a *bad* practice CHIEFLY because the

A. hose is likely to whip about violently
B. hose is likely to burst
C. valve handle is likely to snap
D. valve handle is likely to jam

12. Fire can continue where there are present fuel, oxygen from the air or other source, and a sufficiently high temperature to maintain combustion. The method of extinguishment of fire MOST commonly used is to

A. remove the fuel
B. exclude the oxygen from the burning material
C. reduce the temperature of the burning material
D. smother the flames of the burning material

13.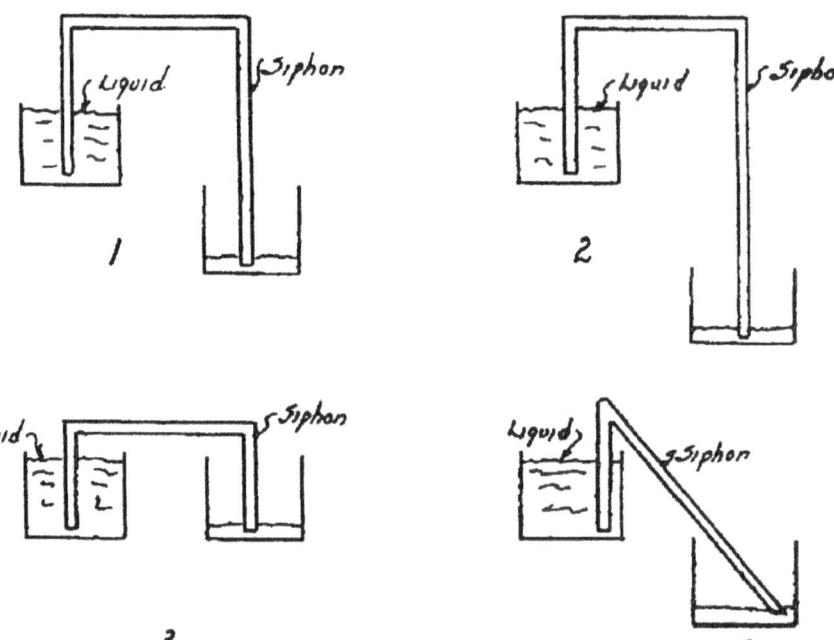

The one of the siphon arrangements shown above which would MOST quickly transfer a solution from the container on the left side to the one on the right side is numbered

A. 1   B. 2   C. 3   D. 4

14. Static electricity is a hazard in industry CHIEFLY because it may cause

A. dangerous or painful burns
B. chemical decomposition of toxic elements
C. sparks which can start an explosion
D. overheating of electrical equipment

15.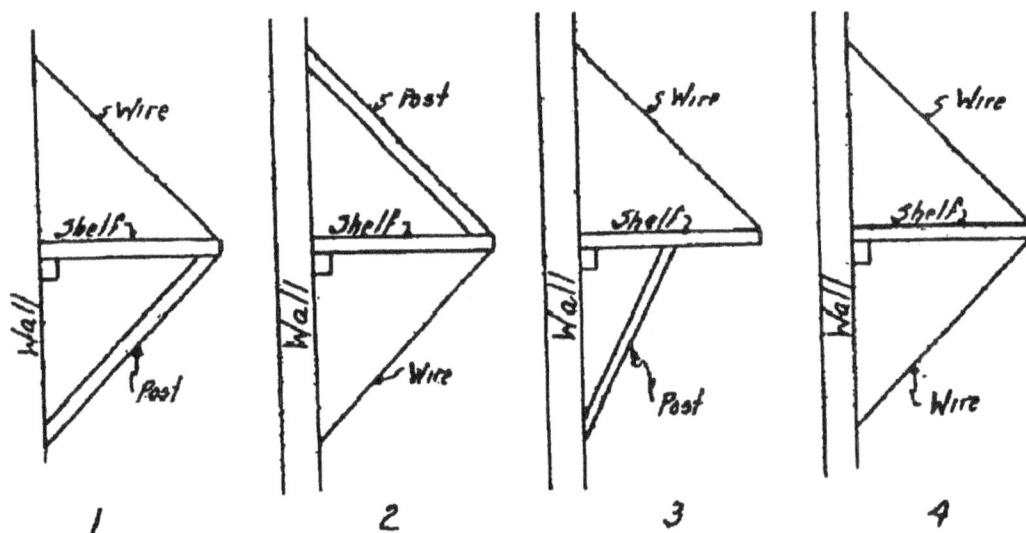

The STRONGEST method of supporting the shelf is shown in diagram

A. 1   B. 2   C. 3   D. 4

16. A row boat will float *deeper* in fresh water than in salt water *because*

    A. in the salt water the salt will occupy part of the space
    B. fresh water is heavier than salt water
    C. salt water is heavier than fresh water
    D. salt water offers less resistance than fresh water

17.

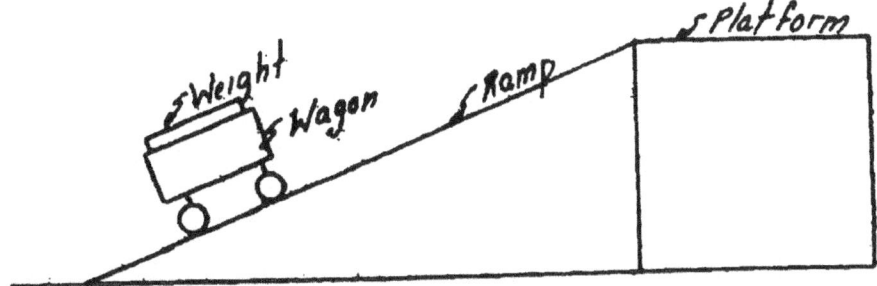

It is easier to get the load onto the platform by using the ramp than it is to lift it directly onto the platform. This is *true* because the effect of the ramp is to

    A. reduce the amount of friction so that less force is required
    B. distribute the weight over a larger area
    C. support part of the load so that less force is needed to move the wagon
    D. increase the effect of the moving weight

18.

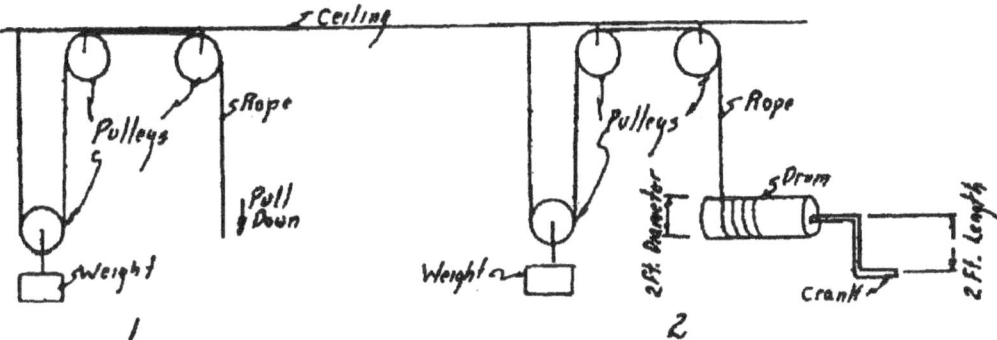

More weight can be lifted by the method shown in diagram 2 than as shown in diagram 1 because

    A. it takes less force to turn a crank than it does to pull in a straight line
    B. the drum will prevent the weight from falling by itself
    C. the length of the crank is larger than the radius of the drum
    D. the drum has more rope on it easing the pull

19.

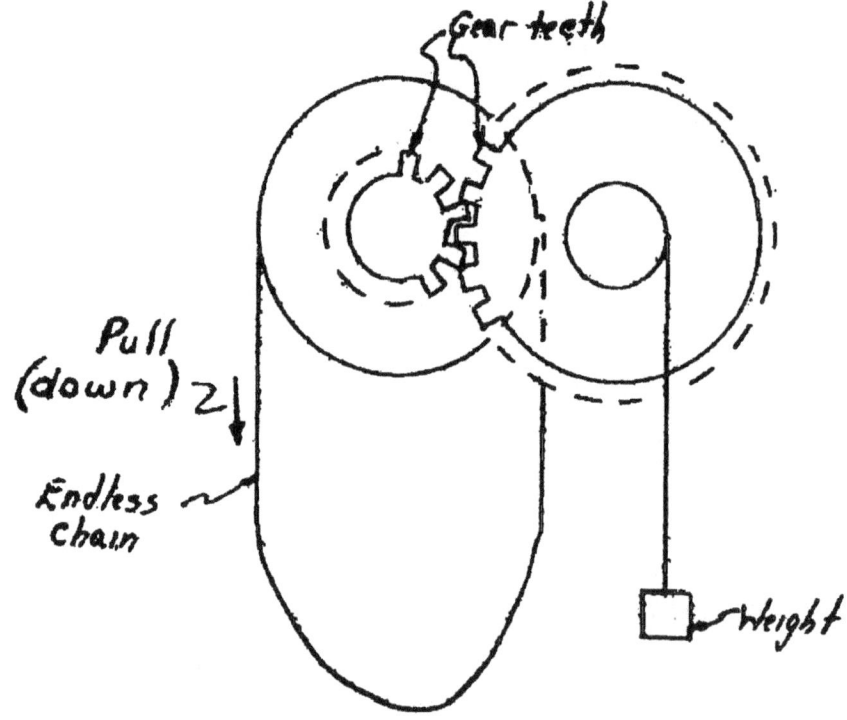

As the endless chain is pulled down in the direction shown, the weight will move

- A. *up* faster than the endless chain is pulled down
- B. *up* slower than the endless chain is pulled down
- C. *down* faster than the endless chain is pulled down
- D. *down* slower than the endless chain is pulled down

20. Two balls of the same size, but different weights, are both dropped from a 10-ft. height. The one of the following statements that is MOST accurate is that

- A. both balls will reach the ground at the same time because they are the same size
- B. both balls will reach the ground at the same time because the effect of gravity is the same on both balls
- C. the heavier ball will reach the ground first because it weighs more
- D. the lighter ball will reach the ground first because air resistance is greater on the heavier ball

21. It is considered poor practice to increase the leverage of a wrench by placing a pipe over the handle of the wrench. This is true PRINCIPALLY because

- A. the wrench may break
- B. the wrench may slip off the nut
- C. it is harder to place the wrench on the nut
- D. the wrench is more difficult to handle

22.

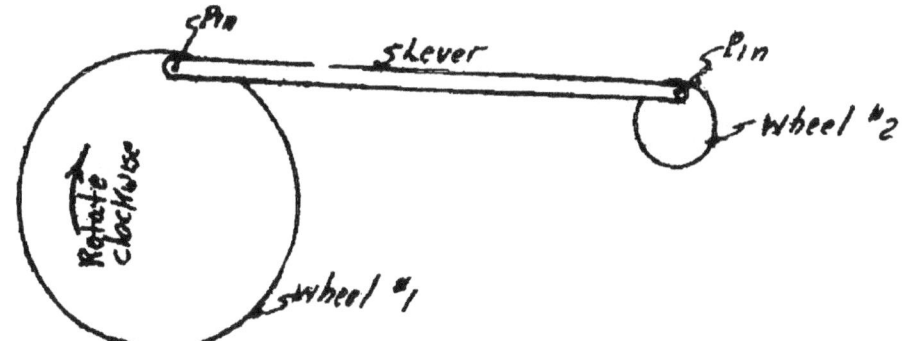

If wheel #1 is turned in the direction shown, wheel #2 will

- A. turn continously in a clockwise direction
- B. turn continously in a counterclockwise direction
- C. move back and fourth
- D. became jammed and both wheels will shop

23. ALL SOLID AREAS REPRESENT EQUAL WEIGHTS ATTACHED TO THE FLYWHEEL

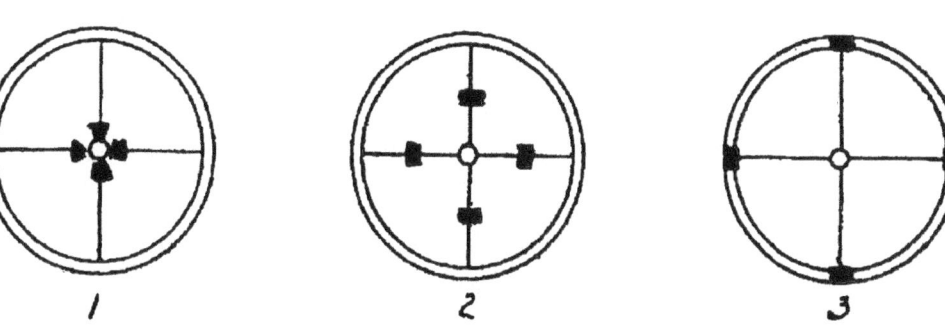

The above diagrams are of flywheels made of the same material with the same dimensions and attached to similar engines. The solid areas represent equal weights attached to the fly wheel. If all three engines are running at the same speed for the same length of time and the power to the engines is shut of simultaneously,

- A. wheel 1 will continue turning longest
- B. wheel 2 will continue turning longest
- C. wheel 3 will continue turning longest
- D. all three wheels will continue turning for the same time

24. The one of the following substance which expands when freezing is

   A. alcohol   B. ammonia   C. mercury   D. water

25. A piece of copper wire 30 feet long is cut into two pieces, 20 feet and 10 feet. The resistance of the *longer* piece, compared to the shorter, is

   A. one-half as much   B. two-thirds as much
   C. one and one-half as much   D. twice as much

KEY (CORRECT ANSWERS)

1.	C	11.	B
2.	A	12.	C
3.	B	13.	B
4.	D	14.	C
5.	B	15.	A
6.	D	16.	C
7.	B	17.	C
8.	D	18.	C
9.	B	19.	D
10.	B	20.	B

21. A
22. D
23. C
24. D
25. D

TEST 2

DIRECTIONS: Each question or incomplete statement below is followed by several suggested answers or completions. Select the *one* that BEST answers the question or completes the statement. *PRINT THE LETTER OF THE CORRECT ANSWER IN THE SPACE AT THE RIGHT.*

Questions 1-2.

DIRECTIONS: Questions 1 and 2 are to be answered in accordance with the information in the following statement:

The electrical resistance of copper wires varies directly with their lengths and inversely with their cross section areas.

1. A piece of copper wire 30 feet long is cut into two pieces, 20 feet and 10 feet. The resistance of the *longer* piece, compared to the shorter, is

   A. one-half as much
   B. two-thirds as much
   C. one and one-half as much
   D. twice as much

2. Two pieces of copper wire are each 10 feet long but the cross section area of one is 2/3 that of the other. The resistance of the piece with the *larger* cross-section area is

   A. one-half the resistance of the smaller
   B. two-thirds the resistance of the smaller
   C. one and one-half times the resistance of the smaller
   D. twice the resistance of the smaller

3.

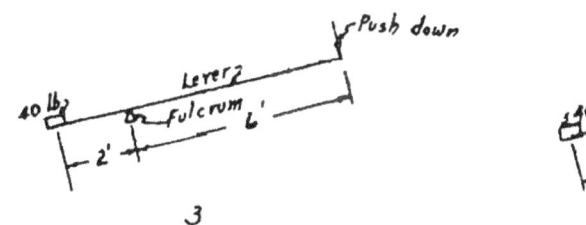

The arrangement of the lever which would require the LEAST amount of force to move the weight is shown in the diagram numbered

   A. 1   B. 2   C. 3   D. 4

4. Steel supporting beams in buildings often are surrounded by a thin layer of concrete to keep the beams from becoming hot and collapsing during a fire.
The *one* of the following statements which BEST explains how collapse is prevented by this arrangement is that concrete

   A. becomes stronger as its temperature is increased

B. acts as an insulating material
C. protects the beam from rust and corrosion
D. reacts chemically with steel at high temperatures

5. If boiling water is poured into a drinking glass, the glass is likely to crack. If, however, a metal spoon first is placed in the glass, it is much less likely to crack. The reason that the glass with the spoon is *less likely* to crack is that the spoon

   A. distributes the water over a larger surface of the glass
   B. quickly absorbs heat from the water
   C. reinforces the glass
   D. reduces the amount of water which can be poured into the glass

6. It takes *more* energy to force water through a *long* pipe than through a *short* pipe of the same diameter. The PRINCIPAL reason for this is

   A. gravity   B. friction   C. inertia   D. cohesion

7. A pump, discharging at 300 lbs.-per-sq.-inch pressure, delivers water through 100 feet of pipe laid horizontally. If the valve at the end of the pipe is shut so that no water can flow, then the pressure at the valve is, for practical purposes,

   A. *greater* than the pressure at the pump
   B. *equal to* the pressure at the pump
   C. *less* than the pressure at the pump
   D. *greater or less* than the pressure at the pump, depending on the type of pump used

8. The explosive force of a gas when stored under various pressures is given in the following table:

Storage Pressure	Explosive Force
10	1
20	8
30	27
40	64
50	125

   The *one* of the following statements which BEST expresses the relationship between the storage pressure and explosive force is that
   A. there is no systematic relationship between an increase in storage pressure and an increase in explosive force
   B. the explosive force varies as the square of the pressure
   C. the explosive force varies as the cube of the pressure
   D. the explosive force varies as the fourth power of the pressure

9.

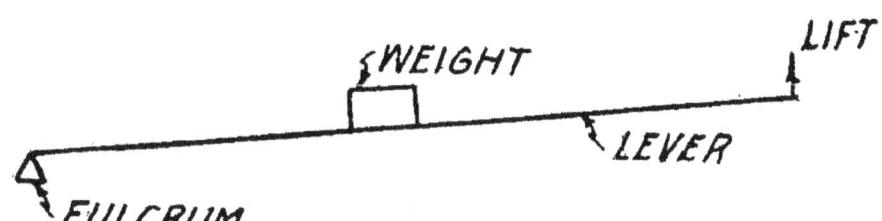

The leverage system in the sketch above is used to raise a weight. In order to *reduce* the amount of force required to raise the weight, it is necessary to

A. decrease the length of the lever
B. place the weight closer to the fulcrum
C. move the weight closer to the person applying the force
D. move the fulcrum further from the weight

10. In the accompanying sketch of a block and fall, if the end of the rope P is pulled so that it moves one foot, the distance the weight will be *raised* is
    A. 1/2 ft.
    B. 1 ft.
    C. 1 1/2 ft.
    D. 2 ft.

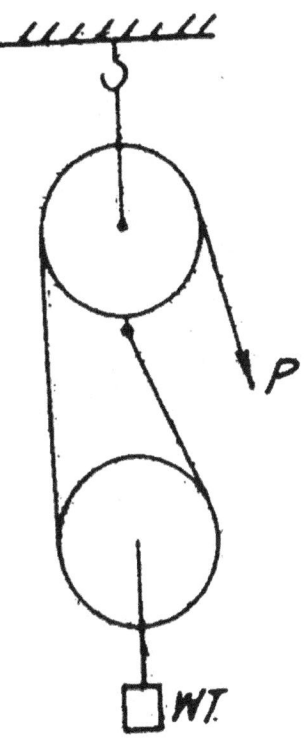

11.

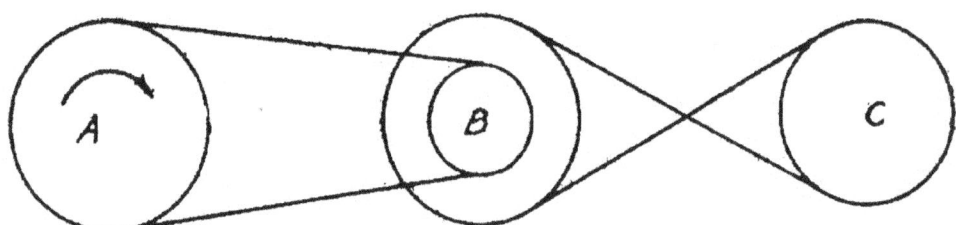

The above sketch diagrammatically shows a pulley and belt system. If pulley A is made to rotate in a clockwise direction, *then* pulley C will rotate

A. faster than pulley A and in a clockwise direction
B. slower than pulley A and in a clockwise direction
C. faster than pulley A and in a counter-clockwise direction
D. slower than pulley A and in a counter-clockwise direction

12.

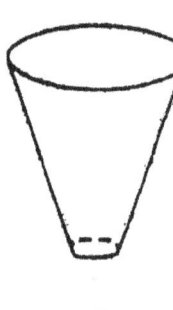 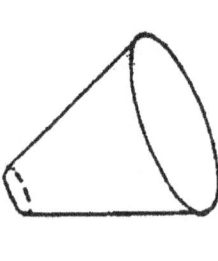 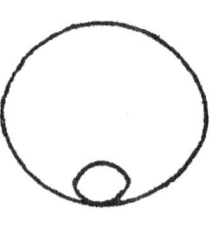

The above diagrams show four positions of the same object. The position in which this object is MOST stable is

A. 1   B. 2   C. 3   D. 4

13. The accompanying sketch diagrammatically shows a system of meshing gears with relative diameters as drawn. If gear 1 is made to rotate in the direction of the arrow, *then* the gear that will turn FASTEST is numbered

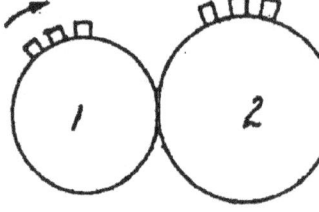 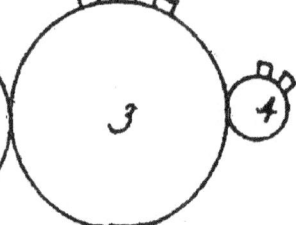

A. 1   B. 2   C. 3   D. 4

14.

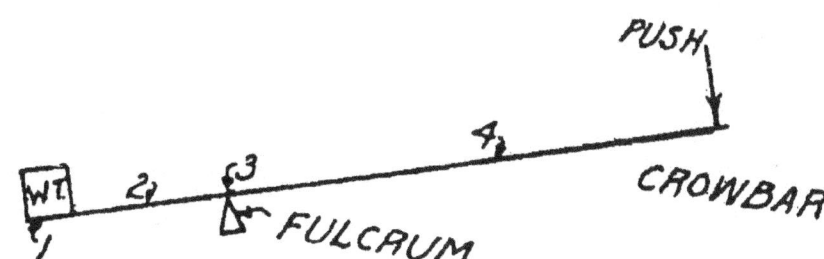

The above sketch shows a weight being lifted by means of a crowbar.
The point at which the tendency for the bar to break is GREATEST is

A. 1   B. 2   C. 3   D. 4

15.

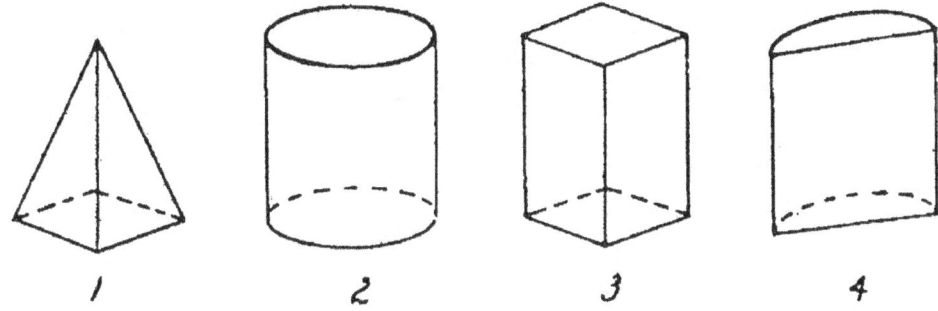

The above sketches show four objects which weigh the same but have different shapes.
The object which is MOST difficult to tip over is numbered

A. 1   B. 2   C. 3   D. 4

16.

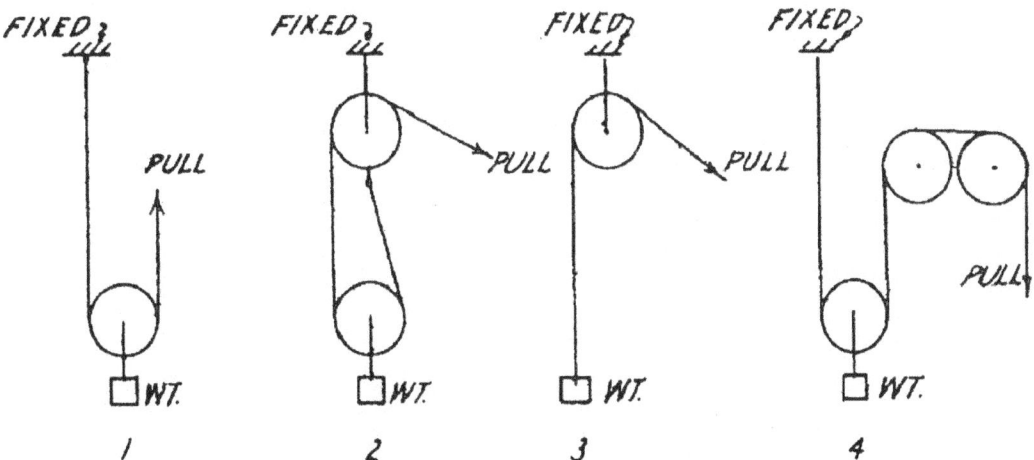

An object is to be lifted by means of a system of lines and pulleys. Of the systems shown above, the one which would require the GREATEST force to be used in lifting the weight is the one numbered

A. 1   B. 2   C. 3   D. 4

17. An intense fire develops in a room in which carbon dioxide cylinders are stored. The *PRINCIPAL* hazard in this situation is that

    A. the CO_2 may catch fire
    B. toxic fumes may be released
    C. the cylinders may explode
    D. released CO_2 may intensify the fire

17____

18. At a fire involving the roof of a 5-story building, the firemen trained their hose stream on the fire from a vacant lot across the street, aiming the stream at a point about 15 feet above the roof.
In this situation, water in the stream would be traveling at the *GREATEST* speed

    A. as it leaves the hose nozzle
    B. at a point midway between the ground and the roof
    C. at the maximum height of the stream
    D. as it drops on the roof

18____

19. A principle of lighting is that the intensity of illumination at a point is inversely proportional to the square of the distance from the source of illumination.
Assume that a pulley lamp is lowered from a position of 6 feet to one of three feet above a desk. According to the above principle, we would expect that the amount of illumination reaching the desk from the lamp in the lower position, as compared to the higher position, will be

    A. half as much   B. twice as much
    C. four times as much   D. nine times as much

19____

20.

20____

When standpipes are required in a structure, sufficient risers must be installed so that no point on the floor is more than 120 feet from a riser.
The one of the above diagrams which gives the *MAXIMUM* area which can be covered by one riser is

    A. 1   B. 2   C. 3   D. 4

21. Spontaneous combustion may be the reason for a pile of oily rags catching fire.
In general, spontaneous combustion is the *DIRECT* result of

    A. application of flame   B. falling sparks
    C. intense sunlight   D. chemical action
    E. radioactivity

21____

22. In general, firemen are advised not to direct a solid stream of water on fires burning in electrical equipment. Of the following, the MOST logical reason for this instruction is that

    A. water is a conductor of electricity
    B. water will do more damage to the electrical equipment than the fire
    C. hydrogen in water may explode when it comes in contact with electric current
    D. water will not effectively extinguish fires in electrical equipment
    E. water may spread the fire to other circuits

22____

23. The height at which a fireboat will float in still water is determined CHIEFLY by the

    A. weight of the water displaced by the boat
    B. horsepower of the boat's engines
    C. number of propellers on the boat
    D. curve the bow has above the water line
    E. skill with which the boat is maneuvered

23____

24. When firemen are working at the nozzle of a hose they usually lean forward on the hose. The *most likely* reason for taking this position is that

    A. the surrounding air is cooled, making the firemen more comfortable
    B. a backward force is developed which must be counteracted
    C. the firemen can better see where the stream strikes
    D. the fireman are better protected from injury by falling debris
    E. the stream is projected further

24____

25. In general, the color and odor of smoke will BEST indicate

    A. the cause of the fire
    B. the extent of the fire
    C. how long the fire has been burning
    D. the kind of material on fire
    E. the exact seat of the fire

25____

KEY (CORRECT ANSWERS)

1. D
2. B
3. A
4. B
5. B

6. B
7. B
8. C
9. B
10. A

11. C
12. A
13. D
14. C
15. A

16. C
17. C
18. A
19. C
20. C

21. D
22. A
23. A
24. B
25. D

TEST 3

DIRECTIONS: Each question or incomplete statement below is followed by several suggested answers or completions. Select the *one* that *BEST* answers the question or completes the statement. *PRINT THE LETTER OF THE CORRECT ANSWER IN THE SPACE AT THE RIGHT.*

1. As a demonstration, firemen set up two hose lines identical in every respect except that one was longer than the other. Water was then delivered through these lines from one pump and it was seen that the stream from the longer hose line had a shorter "throw," Of the following, the *MOST* valid explanation of this difference in "throw" is that the

    A. air resistance to the water stream is proportional to the length of hose
    B. time required for water to travel through the longer hose is greater than for the shorter one
    C. loss due to friction is greater in the longer hose than in the shorter one
    D. rise of temperature is greater in the longer hose than in the shorter one
    E. longer hose line probably developed a leak at one of the coupling joints

2. Of the following toxic gases, the *one* which is *MOST* dangerous because it cannot be seen and has no odor, is

    A. ether
    B. carbon monoxide
    C. chlorine
    D. ammonia
    E. cooking gas

3. You are visiting with some friends when their young son rushes into the room with his clothes on fire. You immediately wrap him in a rug and roll him on the floor. The *MOST* important reason for your action is that the

    A. flames are confined within the rug
    B. air supply to the fire is reduced
    C. burns sustained will be third degree, rather than first degree
    D. whirling action will put out the fire
    E. boy will not suffer from shock

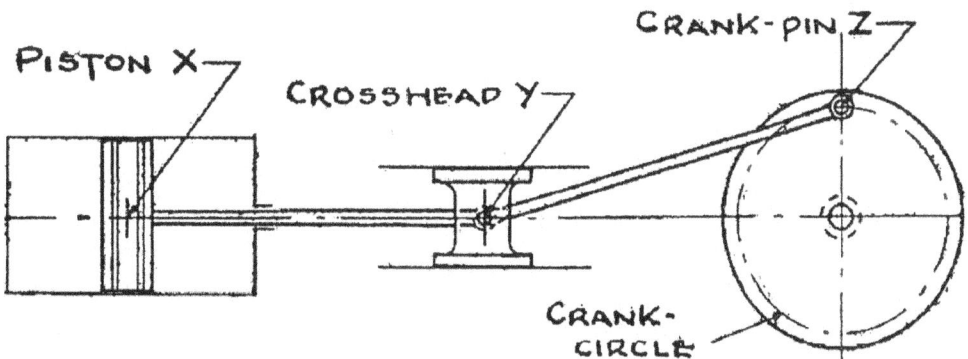

FIGURE I

Questions 4-6,

DIRECTIONS: The device shown in Figure I above represents schematically a mechanism commonly used to change reciprocating (back and forth) motion to rotation (circular) motion.
The following questions, numbered 4 to 6 inclusive, are to be answered with reference to this device.

4. Assume that piston X is placed in its extreme left position so that X, Y and Z are in a horizontal line. If a horizontal force to the right is applied to the piston X, we may then expect that

   A. the crank-pin Z will revolve clockwise
   B. the crosshead Y will move in a direction opposite to that of X
   C. the crank-pin Z will revolve counterclockwise
   D. no movement will take place
   E. the crank-pin Z will oscillate back and forth

5. If we start from the position shown in the above diagram, and move piston X to the right, the result will be that

   A. the crank-pin Z will revolve counterclockwise and cross-head Y will move to the left
   B. the crank-pin Z will revolve clockwise and crosshead Y will move to the left
   C. the crank-pin Z will revolve clockwise and crosshead Y will move to the right
   D. the crank-pin Z will revolve clockwise and crosshead Y will move to the right
   E. crosshead Y will move to the left as piston X moves to the right

6. If crank-pin Z is moved closer to the center of the crank circle, then the length of the

   A. stroke of piston X is increased
   B. stroke of piston X is decreased
   C. stroke of piston X is unchanged
   D. rod between the piston X and crosshead Y is increased
   E. rod between the piston X and crosshead Y is decreased

Questions 7-8.

DIRECTIONS: Figure II represents schematically a block-and-fall tackle. The advantage derived from this machine is that the effect of the applied force is multiplied by the number of lines of rope directly supporting the load. The following two questions, numbered 7 and 8, are to be answered with reference to this figure.

7. Pull P is exerted on line T to raise the load L. The line in which the *LARGEST* strain is finally induced is line

   A. T   B. U   C. V   D. X   E. Y

8. If the largest pull P that two men can apply to line T is 280 lbs., the MAXIMUM load L that they can raise without regard to frictional losses is, *most nearly*, _____ lbs.
   A. 1960
   B. 1680
   C. 1400
   D. 1260
   E. 1120

8_____

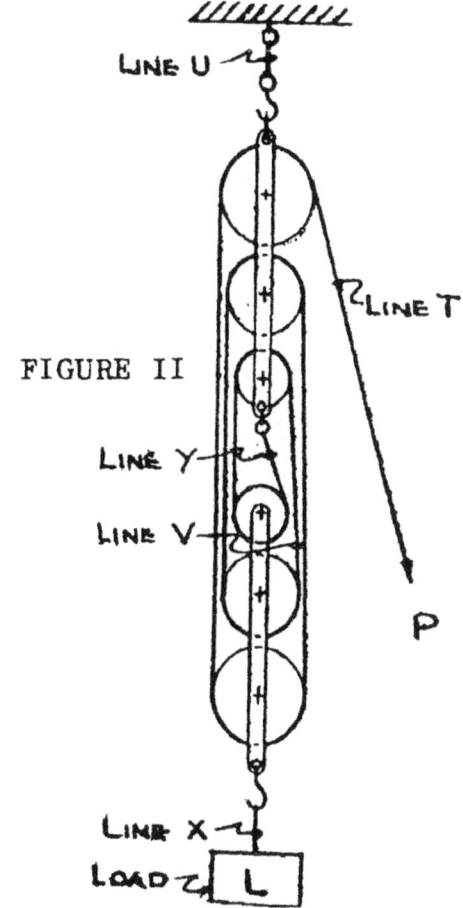

FIGURE II

Questions 9-13.

DIRECTIONS: Answer Questions 9 to 13 on the basis of Figure III. The diagram schematically illustrates part of a water tank. 1 and 5 are outlet and inlet pipes, respectively. 2 is a valve which can be used to open and close the outlet pipe by hand. 3 is a float which is rigidly connected to valve 4 by an iron bar, thus causing that valve to open or shut as the float rises or falls 4 is a hinged valve which controls the flow of water into the tank.

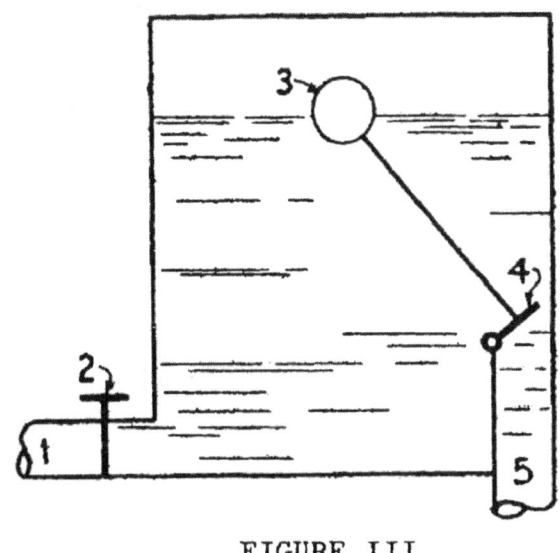

FIGURE III

4 (#3)

9. If the tank is half filled and water is going out of pipe 1 more rapidly than it is coming in through pipe 5, *then*

   A. valve 2 is closed
   B. float 3 is rising in the tank
   C. valve 4 is opening wider
   D. valve 4 is closed
   E. float 3 is stationary

   9 ___

10. If the tank is half filled with water and water is coming in through inlet pipe 5 more rapidly than it is going out through outlet pipe 1, *then*

    A. valve 2 is closed
    B. float 3 is rising in the tank
    C. valve 4 is opening wider
    D. valve 4 is closed
    E. float 3 is stationary

    10 ___

11. If the tank is empty, then it can *normally* be expected that

    A. float 3 is at its highest position
    B. float 3 is at its lowest position
    C. valve 2 is closed
    D. valve 4 is closed
    E. water will not come into the tank

    11 ___

12. If float 3 develops a leak, *then*

    A. the tank will tend to empty
    B. water will tend to stop coming into the tank
    C. valve 4 will tend to close
    D. valve 2 will tend to close
    E. valve 4 will tend to remain open

    12 ___

13. Without any other changes being made, if the bar joining the float to valve 4 is removed and a slightly shorter bar substituted, *then*

    A. a smaller quantity of water in the tank will be required before the float closes valve 4
    B. valve 4 will not open
    C. valve 4 will not close
    D. it is not possible to determine what will happen
    E. a greater quantity of water in the tank will be required before the float closes valve 4

    13 ___

Questions 14-18.

DIRECTIONS: Answer Questions 14 to 18 on the basis of Figure IV. A, B, C and D are four meshed gears forming a gear train. Gear A is the driver. Gears A and D each have twice as many teeth as gear B, and gear C has four times as many teeth as gear B. The diagram is schematic: the teeth go all around each gear.

14. *Two* gears which turn in the *same* direction are:

    A. A and B
    B. B and C
    C. C and D
    D. D and A
    E. B and D

    14 ___

15. The *two* gears which revolve at the *same* speed are gears

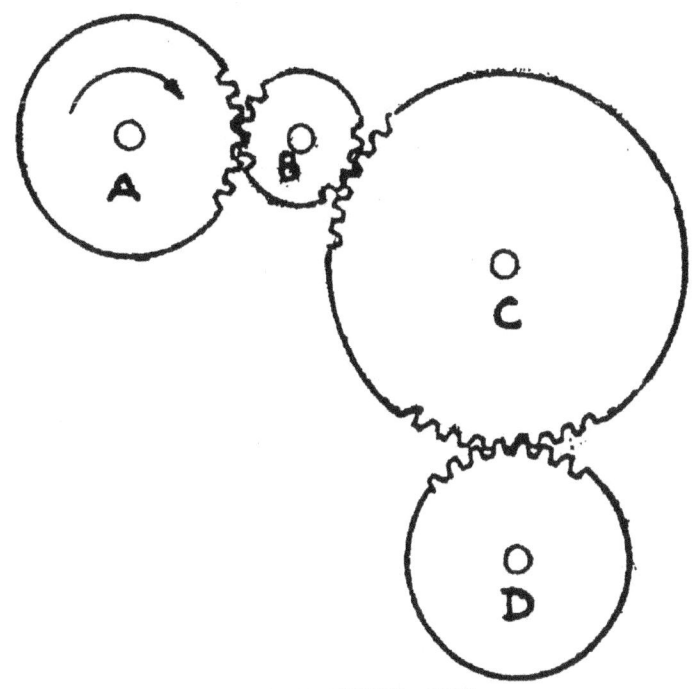

FIGURE IV

   A. A and C   B. A and D   C. B and C
   D. B and D   E. D and C

16. If all the teeth on gear C are stripped without affecting the teeth on gears A, B, and D, then rotation would occur *only* in gear(s)

   A. C   B. D   C. A and B
   D. A, B, and D   E. B and D

17. If gear D is rotating at the rate of 100 RPM, then gear B is rotating at the rate of _____ RPM.

   A. 25   B. 50   C. 100   D. 200   E. 400

18. If gear A turns at the rate of two revolutions per second, then the number of revolutions per second that gear C turns is

   A. 1   B. 2   C. 3   D. 4   E. 8

Questions 19-23.

DIRECTIONS: Answer Questions 19 to 23 on the basis of Figure V. The diagram shows a water pump in cross section: 1 is a check valve, 2 and 3 are the spring and diaphragm, respectively, of the discharge valve, 4 is the pump piston; 5 is the inlet valve, and 6 is the pump cylinder. All valves permit the flow of water in one direction only.

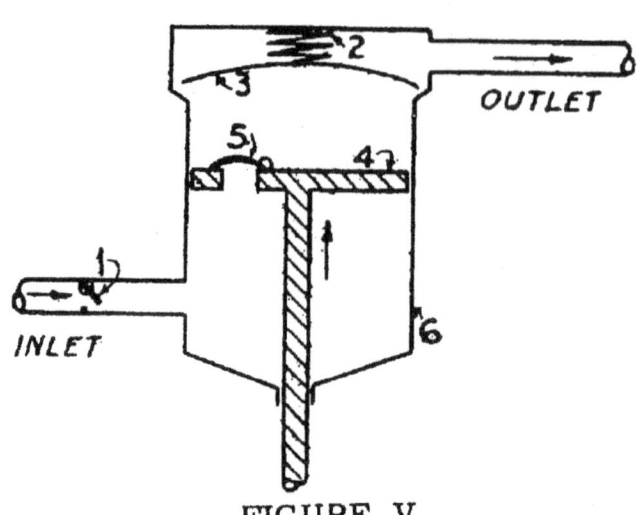

FIGURE V

19. When water is flowing through the outlet pipe,

    A. check valve 1 is closed
    B. diaphragm 3 is closed
    C. valve 5 is closed
    D. spring 2 is fully extended
    E. the piston is on the downstroke

20. If valve 5 does not work properly and stays closed, *then*

    A. the piston cannot move down
    B. the piston cannot move up
    C. diaphragm 3 cannot open
    D. check valve 1 cannot close
    E. the flow of water will be reversed

21. If diaphragm 3 does not work properly and stays in the open position, *then*

    A. check valve 1 will not open
    B. valve 5 will not open
    C. spring 2 will be compressed
    D. spring 2 will be extended
    E. water will not flow through the inlet pipe

22. When valve 5 is open during normal operation of the pump, *then*

    A. spring 2 is fully compressed
    B. the piston is on the upstroke
    C. water is flowing through check valve 1
    D. a vacuum is formed between the piston and the bottom of the cylinder
    E. diaphragm 3 is closed

23. If check valve 1 jams and stays closed, *then*

    A. valve 5 will be open on both the upstroke and down stroke of the piston
    B. a vacuum will tend to form in the inlet pipe between the source of the water supply and check valve 1
    C. pressure on the cylinder side of check valve 1 will increase

D. less force will be required to move the piston down
E. more force will be required to move the piston down

24. The one of the following which *BEST* explains why smoke usually rises from a fire is that 24____

    A. cooler, heavier air displaces lighter, warm air
    B. heat energy of the fire propels the smoke upward
    C. suction from the upper air pulls the smoke upward
    D. burning matter is chemically changed into heat energy

25. The practice of racing a car engine to warm it up in cold weather, generally, is 25____

    A. *good, MAINLY* because repeated stalling of the engine and drain on the battery is avoided
    B. *bad, MAINLY* because too much gas is used to get the engine heated
    C. *good, MAINLY* because the engine becomes operational in the shortest period of time
    D. *bad, MAINLY* because proper lubrication is not established rapidly enough

KEY (CORRECT ANSWERS)

1.	C	11.	B
2.	B	12.	E
3.	B	13.	A
4.	D	14.	E
5.	D	15.	B
6.	B	16.	C
7.	B	17.	D
8.	B	18.	A
9.	C	19.	C
10.	B	20.	A

21. C
22. E
23. D
24. A
25. D

ARITHMETIC
EXAMINATION SECTION
TEST 1

DIRECTIONS: Each question or incomplete statement is followed by several suggested answers or completions. Select the one that *BEST* answers the question or completes the statement. *PRINT THE LETTER OF TEE CORRECT ANSWER IN THE SPACE AT THE RIGHT.*

1. Add $4.34, $34.50, $6.00, $101.76, $90.67. From the result, subtract $60.54 and $10,56.   1.____
   A. $76.17   B. $156.37   C. $166.17   D. $300.37

2. Add 2,200, 2,600, 252 and 47.96. From the result, subtract 202.70, 1,200, 2,150 and 434.43.   2.____
   A. 1,112.83   B. 1,213.46   C. 1,341.51   D. 1,348.91

3. Multiply 1850 by .05 and multiply 3300 by .08 and, then, add both results,   3.____
   A. 242.50   B. 264,00   C. 333.25   D. 356.50

4. Multiply 312.77 by .04. Round off the result to the nearest hundredth.   4.____
   A. 12.52   B. 12.511   C. 12.518   D. 12.51

5. Add 362.05, 91.13, 347.81 and 17.46 and then divide the result by 6. The answer, rounded off to the nearest hundredth, is: 5.____
   A. 138.409   B. 137.409   C. 136.41   D. 136.40

6. Add 66.25 and 15.06 and, then, multiply the result by 2 1/6. The answer is, most nearly,   6.____
   A. 176.18   B. 176.17   C. 162.66   D. 162.62

7. Each of the following items contains three decimals. In which case do *all* three decimals have the *SAME* value?   7.____
   A. .3; .30; .03   B. .25; .250; .2500
   C. 1.9; 1.90;1.09   D. .35; .350; .035

8. Add 1/2 the sum of (539.84 and 479.26) to 1/3 the sum of (1461.93 and 927.27). Round off the result to the nearest whole number.   8.____
   A. 3408   B. 2899   C. 1816   D. 1306

9. Multiply $5,906.09 by 15% and, then, divide the result by 3 and round off to the nearest cent.   9.____
   A. $295.30   B. $885.91   C. $2,657.74   D. $29,530.45

10. Multiply 630 by 517.   10.____
    A. 325,710   B. 345,720   C. 362,425   D. 385,660

11. Multiply 35 by 846.
    A. 4050 B. 9450 C. 18740 D. 29610

12. Multiply 823 by 0.05.
    A. 0.4115 B. 4.115 C. 41.15 D. 411.50

13. Multiply 1690 by 0.10.
    A. 0.169 B. .1.69 C. 16.90 D. 169.0

14. Divide 2765 by 35.
    A. 71 B. 79 C. 87 D. 93

15. From $18.55 subtract $6.80.
    A. $9.75 B. $10.95 C. $11.75 D. $25.35

16. The sum of 2.75 + 4.50 + 3.60 is:
    A. 9.75 B. 10.85 C. 11.15 D. 11.95

17. The sum of 9.63 + 11.21 + 17.25 is:
    A. 36.09 B. 38.09 C. 39.92 D. 41.22

18. The sum of 112.0 + 16.9 + 3.84 is:
    A. 129.3 B. 132.74 C. 136.48 D. 167.3

19. When 65 is added to the result of 14 multiplied by 13, the answer is:
    A. 92 B. 182 C. 247 D. 16055

20. From $391.55 subtract $273.45.
    A. $118.10 B. $128.20 C. $178.10 D. $218.20

KEY (CORRECT ANSWERS)

1. C
2. A
3. D
4. D
5. C
6. B
7. B
8. D
9. C
10. A
11. D
12. C
13. D
14. B
15. C
16. B
17. B
18. B
19. C
20. A

SOLUTIONS TO PROBLEMS

1. ($4.34 + $34.50 + $6.00 + $101.76 + $90.67) - ($60.54 + $10.56) = $237.27 - $71.10 = $166.17.

2. (2200 + 2600 + 252 + 47.96) - (202.70 + 1200 + 2150 + 434.43) = 5099.96 - 3987.13 = 1112.83

3. (1850)(.05) + (3300)(.08) = 92.5 + 264 = 356.50

4. (312.77)(.04) = 12.5108 = 12.51 to nearest hundredth

5. $(362.05 + 91.13 + 347.81 + 17.46) \div 6 = 136.40\overline{83} = 136.41$ to nearest hundredth

6. $(66.25 + 15.06)(2\frac{1}{6}) = 176.17\overline{16} \approx 176.17$

7. .25 = .250 = .2500

8. $(\frac{1}{2})(539.84 + 479.26) + \frac{1}{3}(1461.93 + 927.27) = 509.55 + 796.4 = 1305.95 = 1306$ nearest whole number

9. ($5906.09)(.15) ÷ 3 = ($885.9135)/3 = 295.3045 = $295.30 to nearest cent

10. (630)(517) = 325,710

11. (35)(846) = 29,610

12. (823)(.05) = 41.15

13. (1690)(10) = 169.0

14. 2765 ÷ 3.5 = 79

15. $18.55 - $6.80 = $11.75

16. 2.75 + 4.50 + 3.60 = 10.85

17. 9.63 + 11.21 + 17.25 = 38.09

18. 112.0 + 16.9 + 3.84 = 132.74

19. 65 + (14)(13) = 65 + 182 = 247

20. $391.55 - $273.45 = $118.10

TEST 2

DIRECTIONS: Each question or incomplete statement is followed by several suggested answers or completions. Select the one that BEST answers the question or completes the statement. *PRINT THE LETTER OF TEE CORRECT ANSWER IN THE SPACE AT THE RIGHT.*

1. The sum of $29.61 + $101.53 + $943.64 is: 1.____
   A. $983.88   B. $1074.78   C. $1174.98   D. $1341.42

2. The sum of $132.25 + $85.63 + $7056,44 is: 2.____
   A. $1694.19   B. $7274.32   C. $8464.57   D. $9346.22

3. The sum of 4010 + 1271 + 838 + 23 is: 3.____
   A. 6142   B. 6162   C. 6242   D. 6362

4. The sum of 53632 + 27403 + 98765 + 75424 is: 4.____
   A. 19214   B. 215214   C. 235224   D. 255224

5. The sum of 76342 + 49050 + 21206 + 59989 is: 5.____
   A. 196586   B. 206087   C. 206587   D. 234487

6. The sum of $452.13 + $963.45 + $621.25 is: 6.____
   A. $1936.83   B. $2036.83   C. $2095.73   D. $2135.73

7. The sum of 36392 + 42156 + 98765 is: 7.____
   A. 167214   B. 177203   C. 177313   D. 178213

8. The sum of 40125 + 87123 + 24689 is: 8.____
   A. 141827   B. 151827   C. 151937   D. 161947

9. The sum of 2379 + 4015 + 6521 + 9986 is: 9.____
   A. 22901   B. 22819   C. 21801   D. 21791

10. From 50962 subtract 36197.   10.____
    A. 14675   B. 14765   C. 14865   D. 24765

11. From 90000 subtract 31928.   11.____
    A. 58072   B. 59062   C. 68172   D. 69182

12. From 63764 subtract 21548.   12.____
    A. 42216   B. 43122   C. 45126   D. 85312

13. From $9605.13 subtract $2715.96.   13.____
    A. $12,321.09   B. $8,690.16   C. $6,990.07   D. $6,889.17

14. From 76421 subtract 73101.   14.____
    A. 3642   B. 3540   C. 3320   D. 3242

15. From $8.25 subtract $6.50.   15.____
    A. $1.25   B. $1.50   C. $1.75   D. $2.25

16. Multiply 583 by 0.50.   16.____
    A. $291.50   B. 28.15   C. 2.815   D. 0.2815

17. Multiply 0.35 by 1045.   17.____
    A. 0.36575   B. 3.6575   C. 36.575   D. 365.75

18. Multiply 25 by 2513.   18.____
    A. 62825   B. 62725   C. 60825   D. 52825

19. Multiply 423 by 0.01.   19.____
    A. 0.0423   B. 0.423   C. 4.23   D. 42.3

20. Multiply 6.70 by 3.2.   20.____
    A. 2.1440   B. 21.440   C. 214.40   D. 2144.0

KEY (CORRECT ANSWERS)

1.	B	11.	A
2.	B	12.	A
3.	A	13.	D
4.	D	14.	C
5.	C	15.	C
6.	B	16.	A
7.	C	17.	D
8.	C	18.	A
9.	A	19.	C
10.	B	20.	B

3 (#2)

SOLUTIONS TO PROBLEMS

1. $29.61 + $101.53 + $943.64 = $1074.78

2. $132.25 + $85.63 + $7056.44 = $7274.32

3. 4010 + 1271 + 838 + 23 = 6142

4. 53,632 + 27,403 + 98,765 + 75,424 = 255,224

5. 76,342 + 49,050 + 21,206 + 59,989 = 206,587

6. $452.13 + $963.45 + $621.25 = $2036.83

7. 36,392 + 42,156 + 98,765 = 177,313

8. 40,125 + 87,123 + 24,689 = 151,937

9. 2379 + 4015 + 6521 + 9986 = 22,901

10. 50962 - 36197 = 14,765

11. 90,000 - 31,928 = 58,072

12. 63,764 - 21,548 = 42,216

13. $9605.13 - $2715.96 = $6889.17

14. 76,421 - 73,101 = 3320

15. $8.25 - $6.50 = $1.75

16. (583)(.50) = 291.50

17. (.35)(1045) = 365.75

18. (25)(2513) = 62,825

19. (423)(.01) = 4.23

20. (6.70)(3.2) = 21.44

TEST 3

DIRECTIONS: Each question or incomplete statement is followed by several suggested answers or completions. Select the one that BEST answers the question or completes the statement. PRINT THE LETTER OF TEE CORRECT ANSWER IN THE SPACE AT THE RIGHT.

Questions 1-4.

DIRECTIONS: For each of Questions 1-4, perform the indicated arithmetic and choose the correct answer from among the four choices given.

1. 12.485
   + 347

   A. 12,038   B. 12,128   C. 12,782   D. 12,832

2. 74,137
   + 711

   A. 74,326   B. 74,848   C. 78,028   D. .D. 78,926

3. 3,749
   - 671

   A. 3,078   B. 3,168   C. 4,028   D. 4,420

4. 19,805
   -18904

   A. 109   B. 901   C. 1,109   D. 1,901

5. When 119 is subtracted from the sum of 2016 + 1634, the remainder is:
   A. 2460   B. 3531   C. 3650   D. 3769

6. Multiply 35 X 65 X 15.
   A. 2275   B. 24265   C. 31145   D. 34125

7. 90% expressed as a decimal is:
   A. .009   B. .09   C. .9   D. 9.0

8. Seven-tenths of a foot expressed in inches is:
   A. 5.5   B. 6.5   C. 7   D. 8.4

9. If 95 men were divided into crews of five men each, the *number* of crews that will be formed is:
   A. 16   B. 17   C. 18   D. 19

127

10. If a man earns $19.50 an hour, the *number* of working hours it will take him to earn $4,875 is, most nearly,

    A. 225   B. 250   C. 275   D. 300

11. If 5 1/2 loads of gravel cost $55.00, then 6 1/2 loads will cost:

    A. $60.   B. $62.50   C. $65.   D. $66.00

12. At $2.50 a yard, 27 yards of concrete will cost:

    A. $36.   B. $41.80   C. $54.   D. $67.50

13. A distance is measured and found to be 52.23 feet. In feet and inches, this distance is, most nearly, 52 feet *and*

    A. 2 3/4"   B. 3 1/4"   C. 3 3/4"   D. 4 1/4"

14. If a maintainer gets $5.20 per hour and time and one-half for working over 40 hours, his *gross* salary for a week in which he worked 43 hours would be

    A. $208.00   B. $223.60   C. $231.40   D. $335.40

15. The circumference of a circle is given by the formula $C = \Pi D$, where C is the circumference, D is the diameter, and Π is about 3 1/7.
    If a coil is 15 turns of steel cable has an average diameter of 20 inches, the *total* length of cable on the coil is *nearest to*

    A. 5 feet   B. 78 feet   C. 550 feet   D. 943 feet

16. The measurements of a poured concrete foundation show that 54 cubic feet of concrete have been placed.
    If payment for this concrete is to be on the basis of cubic yards, the 54 cubic feet must be

    A. multiplied by 27   B. multiplied by 3
    C. divided by 27   D. divided by 3

17. If the cost of 4 1/2 tons of structural steel is $1,800, then the cost of 12 tons is, most nearly,

    A. $4,800   B. $5,400   C. $7,200   D. $216,000

18. An hourly-paid employee working 12:00 midnight to 8:00 a.m. is directed to report to the medical staff for a physical examination at 11:00 a.m. of the same day.
    The pay allowed him for reporting will be an extra

    A. 1 hour   B. 2 hours   C. 3 hours   D. 4 hours

19. The *total* length of four pieces of 2" pipe, whose lengths are 7' 3 1/2", 4' 2 3/16", 5' 7 5/16", and 8' 5 7/8", respectively, is:

    A. 24' 6 3/4"   B. 24' 7 15/16"
    C. 25' 5 13/16"   D. 25' 6 7/8"

20. As a senior mortuary caretaker, you are preparing a monthly report, using the following figures: 20.____

No. of bodies received	983
No. of bodies claimed	720
No. of bodies sent to city cemetery	14
No. of bodies sent to medical schools	9

How many bodies remained at the end of the monthly reporting period?

   A.   230   B.   240   C.   250   D.   260

KEY (CORRECT ANSWERS)

1.	D		11.	C
2.	B		12.	D
3.	A		13.	A
4.	B		14.	C
5.	B		15.	B
6.	D		16.	C
7.	C		17.	A
8.	D		18.	C
9.	D		19.	D
10.	B		20.	B

SOLUTIONS TO PROBLEMS

1. 12,485 + 347 = 12,832

2. 74,137 + 711 = 74,848

3. 3749 - 671 = 3078

4. 19,805 - 18,904 = 901

5. (2016 + 1634) - 119 = 3650 - 119 = 3531

6. (35)(65)(15) = 34,125

7. 90% = .90 or .9

8. $(\frac{7}{10})(12) = 8.4$ inches

9. 95 ÷ 5 = 19 crews

10. $4875 ÷ $19.50 = 250 days

11. Let x = cost. Then, $\frac{5\frac{1}{2}}{6\frac{1}{2}} = \frac{\$55.00}{x}$. $5\frac{1}{2} = 357.50$. Solving, x = $65

12. ($2.50)(27) = $67.50

13. .23-ft. = 2.76 in., so 52.23 ft ≈ 52 ft. $2\frac{3}{4}$ in. $(.76 \approx \frac{3}{4})$

14. Salary = ($5.20)(40) + ($7.80)(3) = $231.40

15. Length $\approx (15)(3\frac{1}{7})(20) \approx 943$ in. ≈ 78 ft.

16. There are 27 cu.ft. in 1 cu.yd. To change from 54 cu.ft. to cu.yds., divide by 27.

17. $1800 ÷ $4\frac{1}{2}$ = = $400 per ton. Then, 12 tons cost ($400)(12) = $4800

18. Instead of working 12 to 8, he will be staying until 11 AM, an extra 3 hours.

19. $7'3\frac{1}{2}" + 4'2\frac{3}{16}" + 5'7\frac{5}{16}" + 8'5\frac{7}{8}" = 24'17\frac{30}{16}" = 24'18\frac{7}{8}"$

20. 983 - 720 - 14 - 9 = 240 bodies left.

ARITHMETICAL REASONING

EXAMINATION SECTION

TEST 1

DIRECTIONS: Each question or incomplete statement is followed by several suggested answers or completions. Select the one that BEST answers the question or completes the statement. *PRINT THE LETTER OF THE CORRECT ANSWER IN THE SPACE AT THE RIGHT.*

1. Assume that it takes approximately 1 1/2 minutes to unload a dozen identical items from a delivery truck.
 At this speed, the amount of time it should take to unload a shipment of 876 items is, MOST NEARLY, _____ minutes.
 A. 90 B. 100 C. 110 D. 120

2. Assume that a shop clerk has received a bill of $108 for a delivery of clamps which cost $4.32 per dozen.
 How many clamps should there be in this delivery?
 A. 25 B. 36 C. 300 D. 360

3. Employee A has not used any leave time and has accumulated a total of 45 leave-days.
 How many months did it take employee A to have accumulated 45 leave-days if the accrual rate is 1 2/3 days per months?
 A. 25 B. 27 C. 29 D. 31

4. A shop clerk is notified that only 75 bolts can be supplied by Vendor A.
 If this represents 12.5% of the total requisition, then how many bolts were originally ordered?
 A. 125 B. 600 C. 700 D. 900

5. An enclosed square-shaped storage area with sides of 16 feet each has a safe-load capacity of 250 pounds per square foot.
 The MAXIMUM evenly distributed weight that can be stored in this area is _____ lbs.
 A. 1,056 B. 4,000 C. 64,000 D. 102,400

6. A clerical employee completed 70 progress reports the first week, 87 the second week, and 80 the third week.
 Assuming a 4-week month, how many progress reports must the clerk complete in the fourth week in order to attain an average of 85 progress reports per week for the month?
 A. 93 B. 103 C. 113 D. 133

2 (#1)

7. On the first of the month, Shop X received a delivery of 150 gallons of lubricating oil. During the month, the following amounts of oil were used on lubricating work each week: 30 quarts, 36 quarts, 20 quarts, and 48 quarts.
The amount of lubricating oil remaining at the end of the month was _____ gallons.
   A. 4   B. 33.5   C. 41.5   D. 116.5

7._____

8. For working a 35-hour week, Employee A earns a gross amount of $160.30. For each hour that Employee A works over 40 hours a week, he is entitled to 1 1/2 times his hourly wage rate.
If Employee A worked 9 hours on Monday, 8 hours on Tuesday, 9 hours 30 minutes on Wednesday, 9 hours 15 minutes on Thursday, and 9 hours 15 minutes on Friday, what should his gross salary be for that week?
   A. $206.10   B. $210.68   C. $217.55   D. $229.00

8._____

9. An enclosed cube-shaped storage bay has dimensions of 12 feet by 12 feet by 12 feet. Standard procedure requires that there be at least 1 foot of space between the walls, the ceiling and the stored items.
What is the MAXIMUM number of cube-shaped boxes with length, width, and height of 1 foot each that can be stored on 1-foot high pallets in this bay?
   A. 1,000   B. 1,331   C. 1,452   D. 1,728

9._____

10. Assume that two ceilings are to be painted. One ceiling measures 30 feet by 15 feet and the second 45 feet by 60 feet.
If one quart of paint will cover 60 square feet of ceiling, approximately how much paint will be required to paint the two ceilings?
   A. 6 gallons   B. 10 gallons   C. 13 gallons   D. 18 gallons

10._____

KEY (CORRECT ANSWERS)

1.	C	6.	B
2.	C	7.	D
3.	B	8.	C
4.	B	9.	A
5.	C	10.	C

SOLUTIONS TO PROBLEMS

1. $876 \div 12 = 73$. Then, $(73)(1\ 1/2) = 109.5 \approx 110$ minutes.

2. $\$108 \div \$4.32 = 25$. Then, $(25)(12) = 300$ clamps.

3. $45 \div 1\ 1/2 = 27$ months

4. $75 \div .125 = 600$ bolts

5. $(16)(16)(250) == 64,000$ pounds

6. $(85)(4) = 340$. Then, $340 - 70 - 87 - 80 = 103$ progress reports.

7. Changing every calculation to gallons, the amount of oil remaining is $150 - 7.5 - 9 - 5 - 12 = 116.5$.

8. $9 + 8 + 9.5 + 9.25 + 9.25 = 45$ hours. His gross pay will be $(\$4.58)(40) + (\$6.87)(5) = \$217.55$. (Note: To get his regular hourly wages, divide $\$160.30$ by 35.)

9. $12 - 1 - 1 = 10$. Maximum number of boxes is $(10)^3 = 1000$.

10. First ceiling contains $(30)(15) = 450$ sq.ft., whereas the second ceiling contains $(45)(60) = 2700$ sq.ft. The total sq.ft. = 3150. Now, $3150 \div 60 = 52.5$ quarts of paint = 13.125 or 13 gallons.

TEST 2

DIRECTIONS: Each question or incomplete statement is followed by several suggested answers or completions. Select the one that BEST answers the question or completes the statement. *PRINT THE LETTER OF THE CORRECT ANSWER IN THE SPACE AT THE RIGHT.*

1. A piping sketch is drawn to a scale of 1/8" = 1 foot.
   A vertical steam line measuring 3/4" on the sketch would have an actual length of _____ feet.
   A. 16   B. 22   C. 24   D. 28

   1.____

2. Three lengths of pipe 1'10", 3'2 1/2", and 5'7 1/2", respectively, are to be cut from a pipe 14'0" long.
   Allowing 1/8" for each pipe cut, the length of pipe remaining is
   A. 3'1 1/8"   B. 3'2 1/2"   C. 3'3 1/2"   D. 3'3 5/8"

   2.____

3. Assume that a steamfitter's helper earns $11.16 an hour and that he works 250 seven-hour days a year.
   His gross yearly salary will be
   A. 19,430   B. $19,530   C. $19,650   D. $19,780

   3.____

4. A pipe having an inside diameter of 3.48 inches and a wall thickness of .18 inches, will have an outside diameter of _____ inches.
   A. 3.84   B. 3.64   C. 3.57   D. 3.51

   4.____

5. A rectangular steel bar having a volume of 30 cubic inches, a width of 2 inches, and a height of 3 inches will have a length of _____ inches.
   A. 12   B. 10   C. 8   D. 5

   5.____

6. A pipe weighs 20.4 pounds per foot of length.
   The total weight of eight pieces of this pipe with each piece 20 feet in length is MOST NEARLY _____ pounds.
   A. 460   B. 1680   C. 2420   D. 3260

   6.____

7. In last year's budget, $7,500 was spent for office supplies. Of this amount, 60% was spent for paper supplies.
   If the price of paper has risen 20% over last year's price, then the amount that will be spent this year on paper supplies, assuming the same quantity will be purchased, will be
   A. $3,600   B. $5,200   C. $5,400   D. $6,000

   7.____

8. If it takes 4 painters 54 days to do a certain paint job, then the time it should take 5 painters working at the same speed to do the same job is MOST NEARLY _____ days.
   A. 3 1/2   B. 4   C. 4 1/2   D. 5

   8.____

2 (#2)

9. A foreman assigns a gang foreman to supervise a job which must be completed at the end of 7 working days. The gang foreman has 8 maintainers in his gang. At the end of 3 working days, although the work has been efficiently done, the job is only one-third completed.
In order to complete the job on time, without overtime, the gang foreman should request that he be given _____ more maintainers.
   A. 3   B. 4   C. 5   D. 6

9._____

10. One shipment of 70 shovels costs $140. A second shipment of 130 shovels costs $208.00.
The average cost per shovel for both shipments is MOST NEARLY
   A. $1.60   B. $1.75   C. $2.00   D. $2.50

10._____

KEY (CORRECT ANSWERS)

1.	D	6.	D
2.	D	7.	C
3.	B	8.	C
4.	A	9.	B
5.	D	10.	B

SOLUTIONS TO PROBLEMS

1. 3 1/2 ÷ 1/8 = 28 feet.

2. 14' − 1'10" − 3' 1/2" − 5'7 1/2" − 1/8" − 1/8" − 1/8" = 3'3 5/8"

3. (250(7) = 1750 hours. Then, ($11.16)(1750) = $19,530

4. Outside diameter = 3.48 + .18 + .18 = 3.84 inches

5. Length is 30 ÷ 2 ÷ 3 = 5 inches

6. (20)(8) = 160 feet. Then, (160)(20.4) = 3264 ≈ 3260 pounds

7. ($7,500)(.60) = $4,500. Then, ($4,500)(1.20) = $5,400

8. Let x = required days. Since this is an inverse ratio, 4/5 = x/5 1/2. Then, 5x = 22. Solving, x = 4.4 ≈ 4 1/2

9. (8)(3) = 24 man-days were needed to complete 1/3 of the job.
Since 2/3 of the job remains, the foreman will need 48 man-days for the remaining 4 days. This requires 12 men. Since he has 8 currently, he will need 4 more workers.

10. Average cost per shovel is ($140 + $208) ÷ (70+130) = $1.74, which is closest to $1.75.

TEST 3

DIRECTIONS: Each question or incomplete statement is followed by several suggested answers or completions. Select the one that BEST answers the question or completes the statement. *PRINT THE LETTER OF THE CORRECT ANSWER IN THE SPACE AT THE RIGHT.*

1. Assume that your warehouse received a shipment of 600 articles. A sample of 60 articles was inspected. Of this sample, one article was wholly defective and four articles were partly defective.
   On the basis of this sampling, you would expect the total number of defective articles in this shipment to be
   A. 5   B. 10   C. 40   D. 50

2. Assume that you have been instructed to order mineral spirits as soon as the supply-on-hand falls to the level required for sixty days of issue.
   If the total amount of mineral spirits on hand is 960 gallons and you issue an average of 8 gallons of mineral spirits per day, and your warehouse works a five-day week, you will be required to order mineral spirits in _____ working days.
   A. 50   B. 60   C. 70   D. 80

3. Assume that you work in a one-story warehouse where the total available floor space measures 175 feet by 140 feet. Of this floor space, one area measuring 35 feet by 75 feet is used for storing materials handling equipment, another area is measuring 10 feet by 21 feet is used for office space, and the remaining floor space is available for storage.
   The amount of floor space available for storage in this one-story warehouse is _____ square feet.
   A. 21,665   B. 21,875   C. 24,290   D. $24,500

4. Assume that linoleum tiles measuring 9 inches by 9 inches are packed ten to a box and each box costs $3.50.
   The cost of buying enough linoleum tiles to cover an area measuring 15 feet by 21 feet is
   A. $98.00   B. $110.25   C. $196.00   D. $220.50

5. The number of boxes measuring 3 inches by 3 inches by 3 inches that will fit into a carton measuring 2 feet by 4 feet is
   A. 2,048   B. 2,645   C. 7,936   D. 23,808

6. The stock inventory card for paint, white, flat, one-gallon, has the following entries:

Date	Received	Shipped	Balance
April 12	-	25	75
April 13	50	75	
April 14	-	10	
April 15	25		
April 16			

The balance on hand at the close of business on April 15 should be
A. 40 B. 45 C. 55 D. 65

7. The cost of one dozen pieces of screening, each measuring 4 feet 6 inches at $.10 per square foot is
A. $22.50 B. $25.00 C. $27.00 D. $27.60

8. Assume that it takes an average of ten man-hours to stack four tons of a particular item.
In order to stack 80 tons, the number of men required to complete the job in twenty hours is
A. 10 B. 20 C. 30 D. 40

9. Assume that you are required to relocate 5,000 reams of unboxed paper using only manual labor. The average time required for one laborer to pick 12 reams, carry them to the new location, and store them properly is ten minutes.
In order to complete this relocation task within one working day of seven hours, the MINIMUM number of laborers you should assign to this task is
A. 10 B. 15 C. 24 D. 70

10. Assume that you receive a shipment of 9 boxes of paper towels. Each box contains 6 dozen packages. Each package contains 200 paper towels. The total cost of the shipment of boxes is $64.80. The unit of issue for paper towels is the package.
The unit cost of the paper towels is
A. $.10 B. $.90 C. $1.20 D. $7.20

KEY (CORRECT ANSWERS)

1. D   6. D
2. B   7. C
3. A   8. A
4. C   9. A
5. A   10. A

SOLUTIONS TO PROBLEMS

1. Solve for x: $5/60 = x/600$. Then, $x = 50$

2. $960 \div 8 = 120$ days. Then, $120 - 60 = 60$ days

3. Storage area is $(175)(140) - (35)(75) - (10)(21) = 21{,}665$ sq.ft.

4. $9 \times 9 = 81$ sq.in. $(81)(10) = 810$ sq.in. of tiles cost $3.50. $(15ft)(21ft) = (180)(252) = 45{,}360$ sq.in. Now, $45{,}360 \div 810 = 56$ boxes. Finally, $(56)(\$3.50) = \$196$

5. $(2ft)(4ft)(4ft) = (24\ in)(48\ in)(48\ in) = 55{,}296$ sq.in. Then, $55{,}296/27 = 2048$ boxes.

6. Balance at end of April 13th is $75 + 50 - 75 = 50$
   Balance at end of April 14th is $50 + 0 - 10 = 40$
   Balance at end of April 15th is $40 + 25 - 0 = 65$

7. $(4\ 1/2)(5) = 224$ sq.ft. Then, $(22)(\$0.10) = \$2.25$ per piece. The cost of 12 pieces is $(\$2.25)(12) = \$27$

8. If 10 man-hours are needed for 4 tons, then 200 man-hours are needed for 80 tons. The number of men needed to do the job in 20 hours is $200 \div 20 = 10$

9. 7 hours = 420 minutes and $420 \div 10 = 42$.
   Then, $(42)(12) = 504$ reams transported per day for each laborer. Now, $5000 \div 504 \approx 9.92$, which gets rounded up to 10.

10. $(9)(72) = 648$ package. Then, $\$64.80 \div 648 = \$0.10$

www.ingramcontent.com/pod-product-compliance
Lightning Source LLC
Chambersburg PA
CBHW081823300426
44116CB00014B/2469